# Comptroller's Handbook

A-ABL

I0439154

## Safety and Soundness

| Capital Adequacy (C) | Asset Quality (A) | Management (M) | Earnings (E) | Liquidity (L) | Sensitivity to Market Risk (S) | Other Activities (O) |

# Asset-Based Lending

March 2014

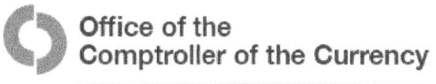

**Office of the Comptroller of the Currency**

Washington, DC 20219

# Contents

# Introduction

The Office of the Comptroller of the Currency's (OCC) *Comptroller's Handbook* booklet, "Asset-Based Lending," provides guidance for bank examiners and bankers on asset-based lending (ABL) activities. The booklet is one of several specialized lending booklets and supplements guidance contained in the "Loan Portfolio Management" booklet, as well as the "Large Bank Supervision" and "Community Bank Supervision" booklets.

The booklet describes the fundamentals and inherent risks of ABL and discusses prudent risk management guidelines and supervisory expectations. The booklet also includes expanded examination procedures to assist examiners in completing assessments of ABL activities. The procedures include an internal control questionnaire and verification procedures to further support the examination process. Refer to the "Glossary" section (appendix E) for definitions of certain terms used in this booklet.

Throughout this booklet, national banks and federal savings associations (FSA) are referred to collectively as banks, except when it is necessary to distinguish between the two.

## Overview

ABL is a specialized loan product that provides fully collateralized credit facilities to borrowers that may have high leverage, erratic earnings, or marginal cash flows. These loans are based on the assets pledged as collateral and are structured to provide a flexible source of working capital by monetizing assets on the balance sheet. While troubled companies often rely on ABL to provide turnaround, recapitalization, and debtor-in-possession (DIP) financing, ABL is also used by healthy companies seeking greater flexibility in executing operating plans without tripping restrictive financial covenants.

The primary source of repayment for revolving ABL facilities is the conversion of the collateral to cash over the company's business cycle. Loan advances are limited to a percentage of eligible collateral (the "borrowing base"). Strong controls and close monitoring are essential features of ABL. ABL lenders may also provide term financing for borrowers requiring longer-term capital or funding needs.

National banks may engage in ABL with no aggregate limitations, provided the volume and nature of the lending do not pose unwarranted risk to the bank's financial condition. Certain limitations apply to FSAs as set forth in 12 USC 1464(c)(2) and 12 CFR 160.30. ABL loans typically would be classified as commercial loans, which cannot exceed 20 percent of total assets provided the amounts in excess of 10 percent of total assets are used only for small business loans as defined in 12 CFR 160.3, "Lending and Investment—Definitions."[1] An FSA, however, might engage in ABL under other authority, depending on the

---

[1] See 12 USC 1464(c)(2)(A) and 12 CFR 160.30. Small business loans include any loan to a small business (defined in 13 CFR 121) and any loan that does not exceed $2 million and is for commercial, corporate, business, or agricultural purposes. See the definitions of "small business loans and loans to small businesses" and "small business" in 12 CFR 160.3.

circumstances.[2] For example, to the extent an ABL loan is secured by nonresidential real property, an FSA may make the loan under its nonresidential real property loan authority.[3]

## Advantages

ABL's popularity among borrowers is attributable to the following characteristics:

- ABL provides ready cash to support liquidity needs, eliminating the need to wait for the collection of receivables.
- ABL provides important funding for companies in cyclical or seasonal industries by providing liquidity during slow sales periods and periods of inventory buildup.
- ABL provides rapidly growing companies the cash to fund growth or replenish internal capital used to fund growth by financing increases in receivables and inventory.
- ABL facilities are typically underwritten with a limited number of financial covenants; the additional risk this poses to the bank is mitigated by conservative advance rates against liquid collateral, strong collateral controls, and frequent monitoring.
- Borrowing terms and repayment schedules generally provide more flexibility and can be customized to fit the individual business requirements or business cycle.
- ABL borrowers in many cases can monitor availability on a daily basis.

For lenders, ABL can be a profitable, well-secured, and low-risk line of business if strong controls are established.

## Disadvantages

ABL can present disadvantages for the borrower and the lender. For the borrower, an ABL facility is often more expensive than other types of commercial lending. Interest rates and loan fees are generally higher and the costs associated with frequent reporting requirements greater (despite this, ABL may be the most economical type of financing available to the borrower). Another potential disadvantage to the borrower is that loan agreements typically allow the lender to take control of the borrower's cash or more readily seize collateral if the borrowing base declines to a level that does not support the loan.

For the lender, the administration and monitoring of ABL is time- and cost-intensive and particularly susceptible to borrower fraud, especially when a business experiences unpredictable cash flow or financial troubles.

---

[2] 12 CFR 160.31(a) provides that if a loan is authorized under more than one section of the Home Owners' Loan Act, an FSA may designate under which section the loan has been made. Such a loan may be apportioned among appropriate categories.

[3] 12 USC 1464(c)(2)(B). This statute generally limits nonresidential real property loans to 400 percent of the FSA's capital.

# ABL Structures

## Revolving Line of Credit

A revolving line of credit (revolver) is the most common type of ABL. The facility allows the borrower to draw funds, repay draws, and redraw funds over the life of the loan. A revolver is commonly used to finance short-term working assets, most notably inventory and accounts receivable. Cash from the sale of the inventory and collection of receivables (conversion of working assets) is the typical source of repayment for a revolver.

A borrower that has substantial working capital needs, such as a wholesaler, distributor, or retailer, frequently uses revolving credit. A service company may also rely on a revolver to fund accounts receivable. A revolver is generally secured by working capital assets, such as accounts receivable and inventory. The value of the underlying assets determines the loan amount and the availability of funds. In some cases, a minimum amount of availability, often referred to as a "hard block," must be available at all times. Typically, a borrower can draw against the revolver as many times and as often as needed up to the lesser of the available borrowing base or the revolver commitment amount. The outstanding balance of the loan should fluctuate with the cash needs of the borrower subject to the availability constraints of the borrowing base. Credit availability is restored when principal is repaid from the conversion of assets to cash and collateral is restored to the borrowing base.

The borrower must comply with the terms and conditions stipulated in the loan agreement, including lender controls and the treatment of cash proceeds, for credit to remain available. In general, cash conversion proceeds are applied to the outstanding balance of the revolver when received. This is commonly achieved through a lockbox arrangement, whereby the lender controls the borrower's cash receipts. The terms of a revolving credit facility can vary considerably. The maturity is typically short term, which allows the bank to reevaluate the risks and adjust the loan terms (commitment amount, advance rate, interest rate, monitoring requirements, etc.) as necessary to reflect the risks. In a growing number of cases, tenors have been extended to as long as five years, which introduces a greater degree of risk if not properly controlled.

An over-advance may be a part of a revolving ABL facility. An over-advance is a loan advance that increases the loan balance beyond the amount supported by the borrowing base. The primary source of repayment for over-advances is typically the company's operating cash flow.

ABL facilities may include a preapproved seasonal over-advance for a brief period during the normal operating cycle when seasonal inventory buildup exceeds sales. In this situation, the bank increases the availability under the borrowing base for a defined period before the peak selling period. For example, a lawn and garden equipment manufacturer may require additional credit availability during the winter months, when sales are slow and inventory is accumulated for spring shipments. Over-advances are also extended for other purposes, such as to take advantage of trade discounts or to finance other assets.

Revolving ABL facilities are sometimes structured with two tranches that each share a senior lien on the collateral but have different repayment priorities. In this structure, the senior tranche is often referred to as the first-out tranche while the junior tranche may be known as the last-out tranche. As the name implies, the first-out tranche is senior to the last-out tranche with respect to repayment and receives all principal payments until the first-out balance is fully repaid, after which principal is applied to the last-out balance. Although the structure may vary, the last-out tranche is typically disbursed all at once with no repayment required until the loan matures or the collateral is liquidated. The last-out tranche provides additional financing to the borrower by allowing a higher overall advance rate while the lender benefits by receiving a higher rate of interest on that tranche.

A revolving ABL facility may also be structured using a second-lien loan to provide additional leverage. A second-lien loan is similar to a last-out tranche in that it is subordinate with respect to repayment, but does not share a senior lien. A second-lien lender's interest is typically governed by an inter-creditor agreement that gives the first-lien lender greater control with respect to the collateral.

### Term Loan

Banks frequently make term loans to ABL borrowers. Term loans commonly finance capital expenditures with the financed assets securing the loans. In ABL financing, however, term loans may be part of a large, structured financial transaction that combines ABL with other secured or unsecured debt.

## Risks Associated With ABL

From a supervisory perspective, risk is the potential that events, expected or unexpected, will have an adverse effect on a bank's earnings, capital, or franchise or enterprise value. The OCC has defined eight categories of risk for bank supervision purposes: credit, interest rate, liquidity, price, operational, compliance, strategic, and reputation. These categories are not mutually exclusive. Any product or service may expose a bank to multiple risks. Risks also may be interdependent and may be positively or negatively correlated. Examiners should be aware of this interdependence and assess the effect in a consistent and inclusive manner. Refer to the "Bank Supervision Process" booklet of the *Comptroller's Handbook* for an expanded discussion of banking risks and their definitions.

The primary risks associated with ABL are credit, operational, compliance, strategic, and reputation. Price and liquidity risks may also be applicable to the extent the bank syndicates or sells ABL loans. Refer to the "Loan Portfolio Management" booklet of the *Comptroller's Handbook* for detailed discussions regarding the role of price and liquidity risk in commercial lending.

## Credit Risk

Credit risk is the most significant risk associated with ABL. An ABL borrower may not be as strong financially as other commercial borrowers, may operate in a highly volatile or seasonal industry, or may be experiencing rapid growth. Characteristics of higher default risk, such as high leverage, erratic cash flows, limited working capital, and constantly changing collateral pools, are common with ABL borrowers.

If properly controlled, ABL can result in lower losses in event of default when compared to other types of lending. ABL's reliance on controls and monitoring, however, can pose higher risk when the facility is not properly underwritten, structured, and administered. Credit risk can be posed by a borrower's inadequate accounting and inventory control systems or poor credit and collection practices, fraud, the failure of a major customer, inaccurate collateral valuation or lack of marketability, prior liens, and other factors described in this booklet.

# Operational Risk

Operational risk is inherent in a bank's ABL systems, staff, and management oversight; a failure of any of these can result in higher losses than other forms of lending. Due to the nature of ABL lending, risk of loss due to operational failure is elevated by inadequate controls for collateral or customer remittances and ineffective monitoring of the borrower's financial condition.

# Compliance Risk

ABL is subject to the same regulatory and compliance issues as other types of commercial lending. Given the emphasis on collateral and the typically higher borrower risk profile, ABL can be more vulnerable to certain aspects of compliance risk, including the termination of credit facilities, debt liquidation, and compliance with state and federal laws and regulations.

## Lender Liability

An ABL lender should monitor a borrower's business very closely. In certain cases, the bank may find it necessary to terminate funding and liquidate collateral because of the borrower's financial difficulties. This can make the bank vulnerable to lender liability suits. Courts have sometimes found lenders liable for contributing to the failure of a customer's business, especially when the lender's actions were considered abrupt or unreasonable.

## State and Federal Laws, Rules, and Regulations

An ABL lender should keep abreast of the various state and federal laws and regulations that apply to ABL. For example, the bank should understand how laws on environmental contamination could affect a borrower and the value of collateralized trade goods. The borrower's financial position could be compromised if the borrower does not establish and follow appropriate policies and procedures governing the generation, handling, and disposal of hazardous materials, where applicable, and maintain adequate insurance to cover the cost of environmental remedies.

As in all commercial lending activities, the bank should be aware of safety, health, and labor laws and regulations that apply to the borrower and could provide an indirect risk to the bank. The costs associated with noncompliance with laws and regulations could compromise the borrower's financial capabilities and ultimate ability to repay the bank.

## Strategic Risk

ABL should be compatible with the bank's strategic goals and direction. A bank's management and lending staff should have the knowledge and experience to recognize, assess, mitigate, and monitor the risks unique to ABL. This requires a continuing investment in the personnel and systems necessary to maintain a sound and profitable ABL operation. A bank's decision to engage in this type of lending without a well-developed understanding of the risks inherent in ABL and a commitment to making the investment required for effective ABL operations poses significant strategic risk.

## Reputation Risk

Actions taken by a bank to protect its interests, such as the termination of a credit line or seizure and liquidation of collateral, can diminish a bank's reputation. Material credit losses may also have a negative effect on a bank's reputation. Failure to meet the needs of the community, inefficient loan delivery systems, and lender liability lawsuits are examples of other factors that may tarnish a bank's reputation.

Some ABL facilities are syndicated throughout the institutional market because of the transaction size and risk characteristics. If the bank fails to meet its legal or fiduciary responsibilities in executing these activities, the bank can damage its reputation and impair its ability to compete successfully in this line of business.

ABL facilities may be part of a complex structured finance transaction. The activities associated with these transactions, as fully discussed in OCC Bulletin 2007-1, "Complex Structured Finance Transactions: Notice of Final Interagency Statement," typically involve structuring cash flows and allocating risk among borrowers and investors to meet specific customer objectives more efficiently. Although the majority of transactions serve legitimate business purposes, a bank may be exposed to significant reputation and legal (compliance) risks if the bank enters into transactions without sufficient due diligence, oversight, and internal controls.

## Risk Management

The OCC expects each bank to identify, measure, monitor, and control risk by implementing an effective risk management system appropriate for its size and the complexity of its operations. When examiners assess the effectiveness of a bank's risk management system, they consider the bank's policies, processes, personnel, and control systems. Refer to the "Bank Supervision Process" and "Loan Portfolio Management" booklets of the *Comptroller's Handbook* for an expanded discussion of risk management.

A bank engaging in ABL activities is expected to establish and maintain written risk management guidelines that include effective loan policies and underwriting standards.

Underwriting standards should address criteria similar to those used for other types of commercial lending, with particular emphasis placed on credit and liquidity analysis, collateral and borrowing base analysis, and collateral controls. The absence of prudent risk management guidelines for commercial lending is considered an unsafe and unsound lending practice.[4]

ABL requires intensive controls and supervision to effectively manage the risks inherent in this type of lending. A properly structured ABL transaction mitigates the risk of default by imposing controls on collateral and cash. The risk of loss may actually be less than with other types of commercial lending, provided that the transaction is appropriately margined against collateral and that prudent monitoring and control processes are in place. ABL expertise, a thorough understanding of the borrower's business, good reporting systems, and in-depth knowledge and evaluation of the collateral are necessary to achieve the appropriate control. The bank should conduct regular borrower reviews and field audits as part of the due diligence and ongoing monitoring processes.

The bank should maintain comprehensive compliance programs that include internal testing and training to mitigate the potential effects of regulatory risks. The programs should cover the laws and regulations pertinent to ABL borrowing.

## Loan Policy

ABL policies should be in writing and initially and periodically reviewed and approved by a bank's board of directors. At a minimum, the policies should address

- ABL goals, objectives, and risk limits and expectations.
- loan approval requirements that mandate sufficient senior-level oversight.
- staff responsibilities for establishing and maintaining sound underwriting standards and prudent credit risk management controls.
- standards for liquidity and collateral monitoring, advance rates, field audits, and loan covenants.
- pricing policies that ensure a prudent trade-off between risk and reward.
- management's requirements for action plans to use when conversion cycles, collateral values (quality of the borrowing base), or operating cash flow decline significantly from projections. Action plans should include remedial initiatives and triggers for risk-rating changes, changes to accrual status, and loss recognition.

## Borrower Analysis

An important characteristic that distinguishes ABL from operating cash flow lending is the reliance on funds provided by the conversion of working capital assets to cash. Key criteria

---

[4] The "Interagency Guidelines Establishing Standards for Safety and Soundness," which describes supervisory expectations for national banks and FSAs, can be found in appendix A of 12 CFR 30 and 12 CFR 170, respectively.

that should be met in order to assess an ABL facility on a "liquidity" basis include

- a properly structured, controlled, and monitored credit facility.
- a facility that is self-liquidating in nature, with minimal reliance on illiquid collateral or over-advances.
- reasonable liquidity and excess availability trends (or in line with plan) with no extraordinary liquidity needs.
- a facility that is stand-alone with a senior lien position and not subordinate or pari passu with respect to other debt.
- reliable projections of future liquidity and borrowing needs.
- a viable turnaround plan, if applicable, with actual performance reasonably in line with plans.

If these criteria are not met, the facility should be evaluated on a cash flow basis. Additional insight into these criteria is provided in the "Evaluating Liquidity" and "Credit Risk Rating Considerations" sections of this booklet.

A bank is expected to evaluate the financial condition of an ABL borrower as thoroughly as any other commercial borrower. To succeed, the company needs to have a plan to establish or maintain profitability and positive operating cash flow. The bank should analyze the borrower's business and industry, including the borrower's position within the industry. The bank should also have an understanding of the borrower's customers and evaluate the quality of the receivables and the level of third-party credit risk they pose.

## Assessing the Borrower's Financial Position

An ABL lender should clearly document and analyze the borrower's financial condition and business operating cycle as part of the credit underwriting and approval process. ABL borrowers may require funding for an assortment of reasons including seasonal working capital needs, growth, acquisitions, and turnaround financing. The borrower may be a healthy company seeking enhanced liquidity or a business that cannot qualify for traditional commercial credit. Most ABL borrowers, however, share a common trait—the inability to otherwise maintain sufficient working capital over the company's operating cycle. Other common characteristics include the following:

- **Excessive debt/financial leverage:** Undercapitalization can have various causes. A company may have lacked equity capital since the company was first organized, experienced rapid growth, aggressively acquired other companies, or experienced large losses that depleted the company's capital reserves. These companies generally have limited access to capital markets.
- **Erratic earnings and inconsistent cash flow:** These are common challenges for borrowers operating in cyclical businesses. These borrowers rely on ABL facilities to smooth cash gaps, and their financing needs are typically counter-cyclical.
- **Negative financial trends:** Occasionally, a bank converts a borrower from a less formally monitored type of commercial loan to a fully followed ABL facility because of

negative trends in the company's earnings, sales, or margins. The conversion affords the bank control over the increasing risk while providing the company with needed credit.

## Assessing the Borrower's Operating Cycle

**Figure 1: Operating cycle**

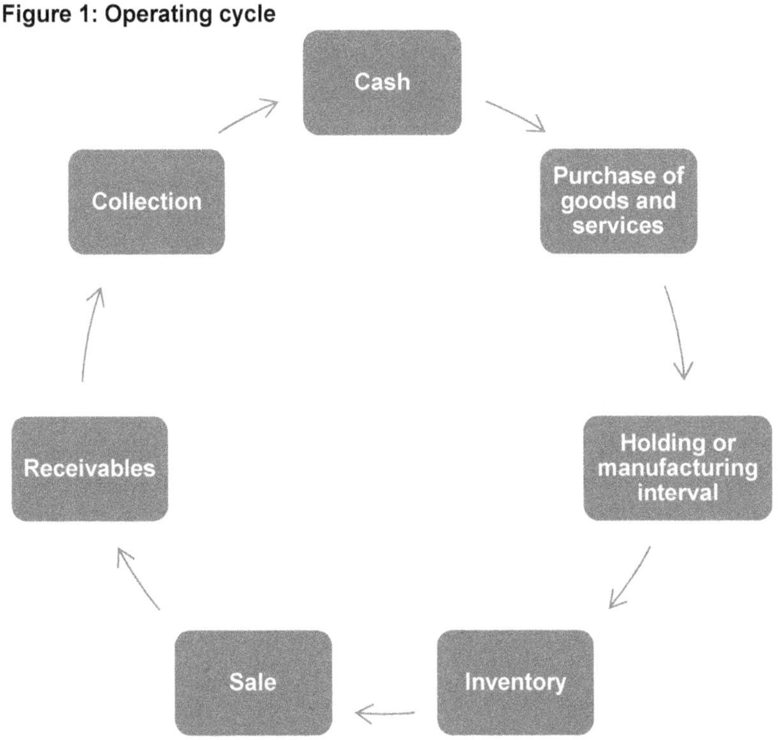

In figure 1, the operating cycle describes the steps a business takes to purchase goods or raw materials, convert those goods to inventory, sell the inventory, and collect the accounts receivable. The operating cycle is generally calculated as inventory days plus receivable days. Operating cycles vary from industry to industry depending on the length of the production process and the credit terms offered. A business must take into account how long after purchasing goods and services (cash outflow) the business is able to convert its own goods and services into cash (cash inflow). A company with a long operating cycle likely has a greater need for financing than a company with a short operating cycle.

A supplier of goods or services may provide some cash flow support by extending credit for purchases. This creates accounts payable on the business's balance sheet. A business may also be able to defer cash outlays by incurring expenses that are not yet paid (accrued expenses). The difference between the cash flow needed during the holding and collection intervals and the cash flow provided by payables and accrued expenses is the net cash operating need, also referred to as the business's working investment need (see table 1).

**Table 1: ABC Company**

The working investment need can be calculated in the following manner.

| Balance sheet (in thousands) | | | | |
|---|---|---|---|---|
| Cash | $60 | | Notes payable | $75 |
| Accounts receivable | 300 | | Accounts payable | 250 |
| Inventory | 500 | | Accrued expenses | 125 |
| Other | 40 | | Current maturities of long-term debt | 150 |
| **Current assets** | **$900** | | **Current liabilities** | **$600** |
| | | | | |
| Net fixed assets | $1,000 | | Long-term debt | $900 |
| Other assets | 100 | | Equity | 500 |
| **Total assets** | **$2,000** | | **Total liabilities & equity** | **$2,000** |
| | | | | |
| **Working investment availability** | | | | |
| Accounts receivable | $300 | | | |
| Inventory | 500 | | | |
| **Op. cycle need** | **$800** | | | |
| | | | | |
| Accounts payable | $250 | | | |
| Accrued expenses | 125 | | | |
| **Op. cycle provides** | **$375** | | | |
| | | | | |
| **Working investment need** | **$425** | | | |

Some analysts prefer to calculate working investment needs in days instead of dollars to facilitate comparative and trend analyses. Refer to appendix A for an analysis worksheet.

## Analyzing Operating Cycle Trends

A business must maintain sufficient sources of cash to meet the business's working investment need throughout the entire operating cycle. A well-capitalized and profitable business can often meet this need from internal operations. A business that has less capital support, is experiencing rapid growth, or has large seasonal demands may require external financing, often in the form of ABL.

Given the emphasis that ABL places on collateral, banks must understand a borrower's ability to convert working assets to cash over a meaningful period. This is commonly achieved through an analysis of the borrower's operating cycle in days, which can be compared to readily available industry data and the borrower's historical performance.

**Inventory Turnover**

Inventory turnover measures how many times a business is able to turn inventory during the year. A high turnover rate is desirable because a high rate implies successful inventory conversion and less likelihood of holding excess, stale, or obsolete inventory. Inventory turnover is a measurement of cost of sales divided by average inventory. A company that recognized cost of goods sold of $150,000 and held average inventory of $100,000 turned its inventory 1.5 times.

negative trends in the company's earnings, sales, or margins. The conversion affords the bank control over the increasing risk while providing the company with needed credit.

## Assessing the Borrower's Operating Cycle

**Figure 1: Operating cycle**

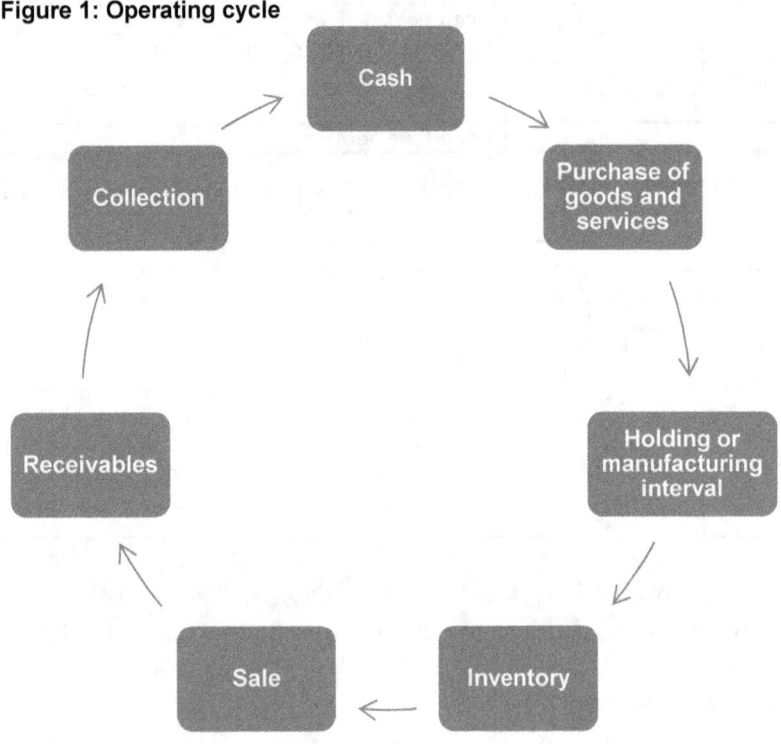

In figure 1, the operating cycle describes the steps a business takes to purchase goods or raw materials, convert those goods to inventory, sell the inventory, and collect the accounts receivable. The operating cycle is generally calculated as inventory days plus receivable days. Operating cycles vary from industry to industry depending on the length of the production process and the credit terms offered. A business must take into account how long after purchasing goods and services (cash outflow) the business is able to convert its own goods and services into cash (cash inflow). A company with a long operating cycle likely has a greater need for financing than a company with a short operating cycle.

A supplier of goods or services may provide some cash flow support by extending credit for purchases. This creates accounts payable on the business's balance sheet. A business may also be able to defer cash outlays by incurring expenses that are not yet paid (accrued expenses). The difference between the cash flow needed during the holding and collection intervals and the cash flow provided by payables and accrued expenses is the net cash operating need, also referred to as the business's working investment need (see table 1).

Inventory days measures the average amount of time inventory is held before the inventory is sold and can vary considerably by industry. An increase in inventory days and inventory days above industry averages are red flags that may indicate deterioration in the borrower's ability to sell inventory in a timely manner. Inventory days are calculated as 365 days divided by inventory turnover. Using the inventory turnover calculated above, inventory days for the example was 243 (365/1.5).

**Accounts Receivable Turnover**

Accounts receivable turnover measures the number of times receivables are converted to cash. A turnover rate at or above industry averages suggests effective collection practices on the part of the borrower. A lower turnover rate may indicate a number of potential issues, including poor credit or collection practices and customer dissatisfaction with the product. Lower turnover lengthens the operating cycle and may increase the borrower's credit needs. Accounts receivable turnover is calculated as sales divided by average accounts receivable. A company that produced sales of $250,000 and had average accounts receivable of $50,000 turned receivables five times.

Accounts receivable days measures the average amount of time receivables are held before they are collected. Increasing receivable days and receivable days above industry averages could be driven by a number of issues and should be thoroughly investigated by the lender. Receivable days are calculated as 365 days divided by receivable turnover. Using the turnover calculated above, receivable days were 73.

**Accounts Payable Turnover**

Accounts payable turnover measures the number of times these liabilities (often owed to suppliers) are paid. A turnover rate below industry averages may suggest cash flow problems or, in cases where performance is otherwise adequate, could signify redirection of cash proceeds by the borrower. Accounts payable turnover is calculated as cost of goods sold divided by average accounts payable. A company that recognized costs of goods sold of $150,000 and had average accounts payable of $50,000 turned payables three times.

Accounts payable days measures the average amount of time payables are outstanding until they are satisfied by the borrower. Increasing payable days and payable days above industry averages could indicate a number of issues, as noted in the previous paragraph, and could ultimately result in loss of critical suppliers or the borrower being placed on a cash-only basis by suppliers. The bank should thoroughly investigate such levels and trends. Payable days are calculated as 365 days divided by accounts payable turnover. Using the turnover calculated above, payable days were 122.

## Evaluating Liquidity

ABL repayment depends primarily on the conversion of working capital assets to cash. The quality and liquidity of the underlying assets are essential to the lender's decision to extend credit. Cash flow from operations is considered a secondary source of repayment for ABL revolvers because the operating cash flow stream is often allocated entirely to cover fixed charges. In some cases, cash flow from operations may not be sufficient to meet fixed charges. It is important, therefore, that the bank performs a robust evaluation of liquidity during the credit analysis process and as part of ongoing monitoring, with proper consideration given to operating cash flow, if available. When analyzing whether liquidity is sufficient, the bank and the examiner should consider the following criteria:

- The quality of the borrowing base and whether the revolver is self-liquidating in nature. Reliance on illiquid borrowing base collateral or over-advances should be limited. The lender should consider the potential for shifts in consumer preferences and the corresponding risk of inventory obsolescence, because ABL losses often result from the inability to recognize or anticipate these shifts in a timely manner.
- The reasonableness of liquidity trends and excess availability under the revolver. Excess availability should be evaluated in light of projected liquidity, provided projections are reliable, and should consider any extraordinary liquidity needs.
- Liquidity coverage of cash usage, often referred to as cash burn. Cash burn refers to the rate at which a company uses up its cash. Cash burn is commonly calculated as the difference between cash inflows and cash outflows for a specified period, though the calculation and adjustments may vary by borrower and by bank.
- When evaluating liquidity, the bank and the examiner should consider whether balance sheet liquidity and excess availability under the borrowing base are sufficient to cover the actual cash burn over the last 12 months. They should also consider whether forecasted balance sheet liquidity and excess availability under the borrowing base are sufficient to cover projected cash burn and other liquidity needs over the next 12 to 18 months. A borrower that does not maintain sufficient liquidity coverage of cash burn will likely be subject to an adverse credit risk rating.
- Whether credit is extended on a stand-alone basis or pari passu with other credit facilities.
- The viability of the turnaround plan for a troubled borrower, including an assessment of actual performance versus planned performance.

## Assessing the Borrower's Industry

Credit performance and the value of collateral can be significantly affected by conditions in the borrower's industry. For example, when the automobile industry is in a downturn, the business of parts manufacturers and suppliers may also slow. Although these companies may have acceptable balance sheets, they may have to adjust for declining volume due to slow auto sales at the same time auto manufacturers are putting pressure on the suppliers' margins. Therefore, the bank should develop a sound understanding of industry risks, including those posed by the business cycle.

The stages of the business cycle can be generally characterized as growth, peak, recession, and recovery. Each stage presents unique risks that can affect current and future borrower performance. The growth stage is often characterized by low interest rates, good credit availability, and consumers with good levels of disposable income. During this stage, a business generally experiences increasing sales, expanding production, and increasing inventory. A business in the growth stage often requires ABL to meet working capital needs.

The peak stage of the business cycle is characterized by increasing interest rates fueled by higher consumer and business spending and generally stabilized prices for goods and services. In this stage, borrower credit needs also begin to stabilize. In the recession stage, production and sales decline, the demand for debt decreases, and business liquidity generally improves. As the stage progresses, a business begins to see new opportunities for growth and increased low-cost credit availability as the cycle transitions to the recovery stage.

The bank also needs to understand the effects of seasonality on different industries. Seasonal influences can increase cash requirements by temporarily lengthening the cash cycle or by increasing daily average sales or the cost of sales. Seasonal sales are usually preceded by inventory increases and followed by a period of high receivables. A company's cash needs begin with the inventory buildup and progress through the traditional operating cycle. Variations in seasonal factors, such as increased demand, can lengthen the operating cycle and increase the company's cash needs. A business may request additional bank debt to meet cash needs. In certain cases, a business may extend payables as a source of temporary cash flow.

An ABL lender may need to rely on a variety of financial statements to determine how seasonality affects cash flow. Annual financial statements alone may not adequately demonstrate the effect of seasonality. Interim financial statements illustrate how sales and working assets fluctuate and, therefore, aid in the lender's determination of financing needs. Interim statements are usually company prepared, however, and more susceptible to reporting errors and fraud. A cash budget can also be a useful tool in determining borrowing needs. Regardless of the type of financial information obtained, the bank should carefully consider the quality of the information during credit analysis and as part of ongoing credit monitoring.

Buyer and supplier concentrations present another form of industry risk a bank needs to understand. The prevalence of concentrations can vary significantly from industry to industry and borrower to borrower. A buyer concentration exists when a company markets its goods to only a few customers, e.g., a niche market. These concentrations can significantly affect cash flow when difficulties arise. A business with limited fixed costs and variable production costs is better positioned to endure the loss of a major customer than a company with significant fixed costs. Concentrations are discussed further in the "Establishing the Borrowing Base" section.

A supplier concentration, where a company has limited sources for needed materials, presents a substantial and often uncontrollable risk to the borrower. These concentrations can jeopardize debt repayment if they cause significant disruptions in the flow of products and services. A borrower that depends on only a few suppliers is more likely to be adversely affected by such a disruption and, in some cases, may even be forced to halt production or service activities. Supplier concentrations should be analyzed as part of a prudent and ongoing credit evaluation process.

Lending to retailers, while profitable and often secured by liquid, high-quality collateral, presents unique risks to a bank if not properly monitored and controlled. A retailer's financial performance is highly correlated to consumer spending patterns (seasonal, back-to-school, etc.) and unique buying seasons that create spikes in cash flow and credit needs. A retailer depends on external financing to manage capital needs during these cycles, and in exchange provides the bank with a security interest in high-quality and liquid inventory. Despite the liquidity characteristics of the inventory, some banks have been reluctant to lend against inventory because changes in the economy and consumer spending habits can cause rapid deterioration in merchandise value. Many banks that have failed to properly structure loans to retailers, monitor the retailers' performance, or monitor the value of the collateral have suffered significant credit losses.

Loans extended to retailers should be structured to allow the lender to react quickly to changes in the borrower's performance or the value of the collateral. Traditionally, these loans have been structured with conservative advance rates equivalent to 80 percent of the net orderly liquidation value (NOLV) of the inventory, as determined by a qualified appraiser, and aggressive collateral monitoring. In certain instances, competition has resulted in higher advance rates of 85 percent to 90 percent—and in some cases even higher, depending on the lender, the collateral type, and the borrower's credit rating. A lender's decision to advance more than 80 percent of the NOLV of retail inventory may raise concerns over the quality of the credit. The bank should clearly document and support such decisions with appropriate risk mitigants.

Some banks institute financial covenants to monitor retail borrowers, but the usefulness of financial covenants is debatable, given (1) the overwhelming reliance on collateral liquidity to repay the debt and (2) a retailer's tendency to experience seasonal losses. Excess availability covenants, however, can help ensure an adequate collateral cushion in the event of liquidation and provide current and meaningful measures of liquidity; these covenants typically require that 10 percent to 15 percent of the borrowing base remain available.

Collateral monitoring is paramount in managing an ABL arrangement with a retailer. Most banks require daily or weekly borrowing base certificates to monitor sales and inventory trends. Supplemental information regarding sales, purchases, and markdown activities is also required as frequently as daily in an effort to identify deteriorating collateral trends as early as possible. This information is particularly useful when monitoring businesses such as grocery stores or discount retailers that sell and replenish inventory continuously.

An assessment of the borrower's merchandise computer systems is integral to the risk management process and should be completed as part of the initial field examination process. Perpetual inventory systems that can report values at cost and by department are preferred. At a minimum, a system should be able to report on key inventory characteristics, including sales, margins, departmental inventory levels, age, inventory roll-forwards, receivable roll-forwards, and data regarding markdowns.

The bank should also monitor the borrower's relationship with critical trade vendors whose behavior can indicate trouble for a retailer. For example, critical vendors can control the borrower's access to inventory and a vendor's decision to suspend supply activities could cause significant difficulties or even force the borrower into bankruptcy. The bank should be

aware of indicators, such as growing payables or slowdowns in inventory purchases, that could signal potentially significant issues and necessitate an exit strategy.

### Assessing the Borrower's Management Team

The borrower's management team is a critical factor in ABL. The bank should thoroughly investigate the company's history and management's experience, integrity, and management style. An evaluation of the company's planning and control systems should be central in the overall evaluation of the management team. The bank should assess management's ability to manage current operations and expected growth. This assessment should be made as part of the original credit analysis and throughout the life of the lending relationship.

### Deal Sponsors

Private equity firms, parent holding companies, and individuals invest in companies that are involved in ABL transactions, acting as the companies' financial sponsors. The parties recognize that ABL provides access to reasonably priced credit and is a particularly cost-effective means of funding buyouts. Sponsorship can provide tangible and intangible benefits to the company, such as access to markets or managerial expertise. Although sponsors do not generally guarantee company indebtedness, a sponsor can provide financial support through maintenance agreements to support deficient cash flows and, under certain conditions, through additional capital support. The ability to provide support, however, can be limited by the sponsoring firm's legal charter, financial capacity, and economic incentive to support the company.

## Establishing the Borrowing Base

In ABL, the outstanding loan balance is limited by both the total commitment of the credit facility and by the borrowing base as determined by the collateral value. Limiting the outstanding balance of the ABL to a borrowing base provides the bank with greater assurance of full repayment from the value of the collateral. Borrowing base monitoring also provides an early warning system against credit deterioration. The increased assurance allows an ABL lender to be more flexible in other areas of the credit process, such as financial covenants.

The borrowing base in an ABL is likely to consist primarily of working assets, such as accounts receivable and inventory. In certain cases, the borrowing base may also include less-liquid assets, such as equipment or real estate, or intangible assets, such as intellectual property, depending on the borrower's credit needs and industry. Reliance on these assets reduces the overall liquidity of the borrowing base and, if material, can affect the approach to risk rating as discussed in the "Credit Risk Rating Considerations" section of this booklet. Regardless of the collateral type, the advance rate should reflect the quality and liquidity of the underlying assets, with lower-quality and less-liquid collateral meriting more conservative advances. The examiner should review advance rates for reasonableness.

## Accounts Receivable

Accounts receivable represent money owed to a business for merchandise or services bought on open accounts. Accounts receivable arise from the business practice of providing a customer a good or service with the expectation of receiving payment at a later date per specified terms. Accounts receivable are self-liquidating and generally collected soon after goods or services are delivered—both desirable traits for a collateral-based lender. The bank must, however, consider a number of factors when determining eligible accounts receivable, including the quality of the borrower's customer base, the presence of concentrations, delinquency volumes and trends, and dilution.

### Quality of the Customer Base

In general, the greater the number of financially sound customers, the better the quality of the borrower's customer base. As the receivable base shifts toward smaller companies, financially weaker companies, or both, the risk increases that the borrower will not be able to collect the amounts owed. Consumer receivables are often considered higher risk because of the difficulties and higher costs in collecting many small receivables compared to collecting a relatively few large receivables.

To determine the financial strength of a significant customer, the bank should review available credit reports, trade checks, and debt ratings, or conduct its own credit investigation. This credit information should be readily available in the borrower's internal credit department. By reviewing the borrower's credit files, the bank can also make sure the borrower has a satisfactory internal due diligence process. After the bank analyzes the borrower's customer base, the analysis should be documented in the credit file.

### Concentrations

As with any credit portfolio, an ABL customer base that has concentrations is riskier than one that does not. A concentration exists when a few customers produce the majority of receivables or when sales are primarily to customers in one industry. Given that many ABL borrowers are manufacturers that sell specialty merchandise or are in the service sector and sell services to other businesses, receivables concentrations occur frequently. A receivables concentration of one account or a few large accounts is often referred to as "single-party" risk; if the "single party" takes its business elsewhere or its financial condition deteriorates, the borrower's business could be compromised. This risk is considerable if the borrower is unable to diversify.

A bank normally considers receivables to be concentrated if there are single accounts representing 10 percent or more of the total receivables portfolio. A bank extending credit to a borrower with a concentrated customer base should limit concentrated accounts to no more than 10 percent to 20 percent of the receivables borrowing base. Alternatively, the bank may reduce the percentage advanced against such concentrations. Exceptions to concentration limits should be rare and based on unique circumstances that mitigate the concentration risk.

The bank should consider the amount of risk posed by concentrations and structure the loan agreement to moderate such risk. In analyzing concentrations, the bank should consider the underlying credit quality of a concentrated customer base.

**Delinquency Status**

The bank should monitor delinquency trends within the accounts receivable base. Rising delinquencies indicate increased risk and may signal problems with the borrower. The effectiveness of the borrower's collection department influences delinquency levels, but other factors, such as an increase in disputed accounts, also can cause delinquencies to rise. Trade terms commonly call for full payment within 30 days of the invoice date, excluding any early payment discount offered. An account that is 30 days or more past due beyond the normal trade terms is considered delinquent. Certain industries have their own conventions. For example, the food industry usually requires payment in seven to 10 days. Normally, an account is considered ineligible collateral when it is past due by three times the terms, e.g., 90 days for 30-day terms and 21 days for seven-day terms. Accounts delinquent to this extent and not excluded from the borrowing base should raise examiner concern. In addition, most underwriting agreements specify that all of a party's accounts are designated ineligible collateral when any (or some percentage) of that customer's receivables become ineligible. This is referred to as cross-aging.

**Dilution**

An ABL borrower and its bank are exposed to dilution risk, which is characterized by the possibility that noncash credits will reduce (dilute) the accounts receivable balance. Returns and allowances, disputes, bad debts, and other credit offsets create dilution. Dilution varies by industry but is usually expected to be 5 percent or less of receivables.

The bank should carefully analyze trends or significant changes in dilution rates, and a field auditor should review and test selected credit memos. These reviews are important because a rise in dilution rates can signal a decline in product or service quality, which can lead to financial problems for the borrower.

**Advance Rates and Ineligible Receivables**

Advance rates for accounts receivable vary depending on the quality and nature of the receivable and the bank's risk appetite. Common advance rates range from 70 percent to 85 percent of eligible accounts receivable. Some banks establish advance rates of up to 90 percent of eligible business-to-business accounts receivable. These banks' effective advance rates are often lower after subtracting historic dilution and minimum reserve levels.

The definition of eligible receivables is also likely to vary depending on the borrower's financial condition, the quality of the collateral, the industry, and the bank's risk appetite. In general, to be considered eligible, the receivable must be generated in the ordinary course of business and be subject to a perfected first-priority security interest in favor of the bank.

The following are characteristics of receivables commonly designated as ineligible:

- Receivables delinquent for a period that calls into question the receivables' collectability.
- Receivables that exceed concentration limits.
- Affiliate receivables that may deteriorate simultaneously. Affiliate receivables can also increase the potential for fraud, particularly in times of financial stress.
- Re-aged receivables for which the probability of collection is reduced.
- Government receivables of the Assignment of Claims Act of 1940, because of the unique perfection and documentation requirements. A government entity also typically has liberal rights to return goods, and government receivables' payment terms often exceed normal trade terms. A bank that considers government receivables eligible should have evidence that the government entity has established an acceptable payment pattern and that the borrower can meet the performance requirements of the contract.
- Foreign receivables with legal, price, and country risks that can disrupt payment. A bank that permits foreign receivables to be eligible often requires a letter of credit or an insurance policy carrying minimal deductibles.
- Contra-accounts (in which a borrower sells to and purchases from the same customer), because the customer can "set off" the debt it owes against the debt owed to it and pay only the net amount.
- Receivables owed by an insolvent borrower.
- Unbilled accounts receivable.

A loan with an advance rate higher than industry norms or historical benchmarks, or a borrowing base that includes receivables generally classified as ineligible, has heightened risk. The examiner should evaluate mitigating factors to the increased risk and assess the borrower's overall condition. A bank often raises advance rates to accommodate a borrower's need for more working capital. Very low advance rates may also warrant added scrutiny because an ABL lender often reduces advance rates to build a collateral cushion if the bank thinks liquidation may be imminent.

Issues regarding the quality of accounts receivable, concerns regarding the customer base, or liberal accounts receivable underwriting practices by the borrower should be reflected in the ABL's structure, terms, controls, and monitoring practices.

## Inventory

A bank should evaluate inventory as it evaluates receivables to establish advance rates. Advance rates on inventory are usually lower than those on receivables, because inventory is less liquid. An outstanding account need only be collected; a good in inventory may need to be finished and must be sold and paid for. An additional risk factor in lending against inventory is the potential for a priority claim by the supplier of the inventory goods. In some industries and states, the seller of the inventory may have an automatic prior lien (also known as a purchase money security interest) on that inventory even if there is no Uniform Commercial Code (UCC) filing.

A bank typically advances up to 65 percent of the book value of eligible inventory, or 80 percent of the NOLV. When establishing inventory long-term value rates, the bank can limit risk by using the liquidation value (rather than the higher market value) of the inventory pledged and by building in a sufficient margin to protect against price risk and marketing and administrative costs. To establish the value of various types of inventory, the bank should rely on expert appraisals or evaluations and the bank's own experience liquidating similar types of inventory.

Inventory advance rates vary depending on the inventory type—i.e., raw materials, work-in-process, or finished goods. Finished goods and commodity-like raw materials usually receive the highest advance rates because they are easiest to sell. Advance rates for some finished products, such as fungible goods or goods with established markets, are normally of greater value than specialized or perishable goods, unless such goods are adequately insured. For raw materials, commodity items, such as iron ore used by a steelmaker, are much easier to resell than customized items, such as specialty pigments used to manufacture paint, which may have only nominal resale value. Work-in-process has limited liquidation value because it requires additional production inputs to become salable merchandise and is frequently excluded from the collateral used to determine the borrowing base.

Inventory must be salable and subject to a perfected first-priority interest in favor of the bank to become eligible collateral. Some inventory should be excluded from collateral because of age or some other measure of obsolescence. The bank should pay particular attention to a borrower in a fashion-sensitive industry to ensure that obsolete inventory is written off in a timely manner. Eligibility may also be limited because of the location of the goods. For example, eligible inventory may be limited to goods located at one location and exclude inventory held at another. Inventory stored in multiple locations may be assigned a lower advance rate because such inventory is more difficult to monitor and control and often more costly to liquidate. Consignment goods are considered ineligible because they are owned by another party. The examiner should apply the same approach to inventory that he or she applies to receivables: assess the reasonableness of advance rates by comparing such rates over time and reviewing trends in similar industries.

Although considerable reliance on inventory in the borrowing base may be appropriate depending on the nature of the borrower's business, an ABL borrowing base usually is heavily skewed toward accounts receivable, and loan agreements may impose limits on the amount of inventory in the borrowing base. The examiner should be alert for a borrowing base that shifts from reliance on accounts receivable to reliance on inventory. This is often a sign of financial deterioration and potential collection problems.

## Other Collateral

To the extent possible, an ABL facility should be supported by working assets. In certain cases, an ABL borrowing base may include fixed assets, such as equipment and real estate, or even certain intangibles, such as intellectual property. A bank that finances distressed companies or acquisitions is more likely to include this less-liquid collateral when calculating the borrowing base. Such an agreement generally limits the less-liquid collateral to a small percentage of the borrowing base.

An ABL facility seldom finances perishable inventory. Perishable items require extra care to preserve their value, must be turned frequently, and have a shorter window for liquidation. In the event of a bank liquidation, the lender is responsible for maintaining the condition of the inventory until it is sold. The costs associated with preserving the value of and liquidating the collateral can significantly affect loan satisfaction.

**Intellectual Property**

A typical company's asset base consists primarily of working assets, equipment, and real estate, but advances in technology and marketing have resulted in a significant increase in intangible assets, most notably intellectual property. This increase has spurred financing interest from borrowers and lenders alike. ABL lenders, in particular, are originating increasing volumes of loans secured by intellectual property, including patents, trademarks, and copyrights.

A bank that engages in intellectual property financing must maintain effective procedures to establish ownership of, and perfect a security interest in, the specific type of intellectual property. Verifying ownership of intellectual property can be time-consuming and expensive. In many cases, the bank must review filings with federal agencies such as the U.S. Patent and Trademark Office or the U.S. Copyright Office.

Perfecting a security interest in intellectual property can be challenging. Most types of intellectual property are governed by federal laws that did not originally consider the practical requirements of financing transactions and have not been amended to do so. Article 9 of the UCC governs the method of perfecting security interests in personal property, which includes intellectual property; however, the UCC is implemented at the state level, and requirements in different states may vary. As a result, consistent practices for perfecting a security interest in intellectual property have not been established. Given this uncertainty, the bank should consult legal counsel when establishing collateral perfection procedures for intellectual property. In certain cases it may be necessary to file at the federal level (e.g., with the U.S. Patent and Trademark Office) and at the state level with a UCC–1 financing statement.

Intellectual property can add significant value to a collateral package or, in certain cases, it can be valuable enough to stand alone as collateral. Valuing intellectual property can be difficult, however, and valuation may require the services of a specialized appraiser. Lenders that finance intellectual property need to maintain appropriate collateral valuation procedures for the type of lending conducted, including appropriate third-party due diligence procedures for selecting outside appraisers. Appropriate advance rates should be established; advance rates for intellectual property are generally less than those for other types of collateral, such as accounts receivable.

## Reserves

Most ABL agreements grant the lender the right to establish reserves against the borrowing base. Reserves are deductions from the collateral value that consider the costs required to liquidate the collateral, the possible dilution of accounts, inventory obsolescence, or other factors that could affect the collectability of the underlying assets. Such reserves are important because they reduce the probability that credit extensions will exceed the proceeds that may be generated through liquidation.

# Term Loans

Before extending a term loan to an ABL borrower, a bank should determine that cash flow from operations is adequate to service both the term loan and the interest-only requirements of the asset-based revolver. An examiner should be aware that even when a term loan is well structured and has adequate collateral coverage, the presence of such debt could increase the risk in the revolver. For example, when a borrower's financial condition is deteriorating, a term loan may call for a different collection strategy than the strategy employed for a revolver. The bank may hesitate to liquidate the revolver if doing so could jeopardize the recovery of the term loan; seizure and liquidation of a company's working assets could disrupt cash flow from operations, the primary source of repayment for the term loan. Additionally, when a loan has cross-collateral features, the revolver's collateral could be extended to cover partially secured facilities, causing the revolver itself to become partially or completely unsecured.

# Controls

## Loan Agreements

The loan agreement should clearly define the terms and conditions of the transaction, including the assets securing the loan and collateral controls. The loan agreement should define the borrowing base, the availability formula, the quality and frequency of documentation used to support the borrowing base, and how cash proceeds are handled. It should also describe the procedures the lender will use to monitor the value of the collateral. Most ABL loan agreements also establish what protections (e.g., insurance and inspections) the lender requires to protect the value of the collateral.

## Collateral Liens

As previously stated, the most common collateral are receivables and inventory, although in some cases, equipment, real estate, or intangibles such as patents or trademarks may be included. A collateral lien should be drafted in conformance with revised Article 9 of the UCC as enacted in the applicable state. Because of the continual turnover of receivables and inventory, the bank must protect itself from potential losses by using specific, enforceable language in the collateral documents. To ensure the priority of the bank's lien position, the bank should conduct a lien search before the initial funding of an ABL facility and periodically thereafter.

Ideally, one bank is the exclusive lender against the receivables and inventory. Sometimes, however, a bank makes a loan against a portion of a borrower's receivables or inventory, and another lender advances funds on the balance of those assets. This type of arrangement significantly increases risk because ownership and control of the collateral among the lenders can be uncertain. It is often impossible to clearly identify the secured interest in receivables among lenders when those obligations are due from common customers. Likewise, it is difficult to separate inventory among lienholders. A bank that accepts this additional risk should take precautions to make commingling of collateral difficult or impossible. At times, a supplier may file a purchase money security interest in raw materials or component parts. This too can compromise the bank's collateral position.

Frequent field audits and detailed collateral descriptions can help reduce the risks, but the best solution is for a lender to ensure that it is the only lender to hold a lien against a firm's accounts receivable or inventory. When there are multiple lenders, the lenders are often forced to resolve ownership issues through litigation. Not only must each lender absorb the expense of litigation, but each lender may also be forced to compromise with the other lenders in a manner that is not totally satisfactory to anyone.

## Collateral Appraisals

Collateral appraisals are important aspects of ABL underwriting, administration, and problem loan management. A bank should obtain an appraisal during the underwriting process to determine the value of the underlying collateral and help establish the borrowing base and advance rates. Updated appraisals should be obtained throughout the life of the loan to monitor the collateral value, collateral trends, and adequacy of the borrowing base. Reappraisal should be permitted by the loan agreement and occur on a regular basis consistent with the risk inherent in the lending relationship. In particular, the frequency of reappraisal should increase as issues arise.

An ABL lender typically relies on expert appraisals or valuations performed by companies experienced in inventory and other asset liquidation. The appraisals should provide a NOLV as the standard for collateral valuation, not cost or retail value. The bank's experience in liquidating similar types of collateral should also be considered.

## Field Audits

Field audits are integral to monitoring and controlling ABL. A field audit helps detect fraud and financial weakness and is a customary way to confirm the quality of the borrower's financial data, receivables, inventory, and internal controls.

The field auditor should obtain written account verifications and perform sufficient reconciliations and testing to ensure that the borrower's financial records are accurate. Testing financial records involves reviewing borrowing base collateral—physically inspecting the collateral, testing its validity and value as reported on financial statements and borrowing base certificates, and examining original invoices and other supporting documentation. During the field audit, the auditor should carefully review credit memo documentation, testing for both reasonableness and accuracy. A field audit is usually the best means of evaluating internal controls, information systems, and operating systems. The audit should confirm that the borrower's accounting systems are adequate. Some banks require independent audited opinions of the borrower's operating and internal control systems.

A field audit should be conducted before a new account is booked and regularly thereafter—often quarterly but more frequently if risk dictates. In a high-risk relationship or workout situation, weekly or daily audits may be appropriate. The examiner should review how the bank determines the frequency and scope of field audits, paying special attention to an ABL unit that delays audits or extends audit cycles because of staffing shortages. An ABL unit should have dedicated field audit staff that includes skilled accountants.

A bank that does not have dedicated field audit staff should still inspect collateral and review supporting documentation periodically. Smaller banks may have staff lenders that are independent of the transaction perform the audit; others outsource. Regardless, the cost is generally passed on to the borrower.

## Financial Reporting Requirements

The type and frequency of financial reporting should depend on how much credit risk the borrower poses. An ABL lender often requires borrowing base certificates and supporting documentation on a weekly or monthly basis. Interim financial statements may also be required; these can help the bank determine whether uncollected receivables and obsolete inventory have been identified and appropriately reported on the balance sheet. In some cases, the bank may waive requirements for interim statements if collateral reporting (borrowing base certificates, receivable agings, etc.) is reliable and field audits are completed on a regular basis without significant findings. The bank's policies and procedures should address reporting requirements and permissible exceptions.

The frequency of reports on inventory depends on the bank's assessment of the borrower's operations, the nature of the inventory, and the reliance on inventory in the borrowing base. Normally, the borrower should be required to periodically certify the amount, type, and condition of inventory; provide inventory valuations; and permit the lender or an independent firm to audit the inventory.

## Covenants

Loan agreements typically include multiple financial covenants that require the borrower to maintain or achieve certain financial ratios or other financial performance metrics as an ongoing condition of credit. The covenants not only establish standards for financial performance, they also serve as early indicators of potential problems and provide the bank with default triggers that force restructuring or other remedial actions that can moderate the risk of loss. Covenants can also be used as tools to limit a borrower's capacity to take unwarranted risks.

The use of covenants in ABL differs from traditional commercial lending. An ABL lender places less reliance on financial covenants and more reliance on collateral controls and monitoring. This is a significant benefit to an ABL borrower that may be experiencing rapid growth or financial challenges. Covenants commonly focus on excess availability and may take the form of a reserve against the borrowing base and cash controls, such as cash dominion using a lockbox arrangement. Financial covenants, when present, typically take the form of a minimum fixed charge coverage ratio, the definition of which can vary by borrower. Limits on capital expenditures are also common in ABL. Covenants should be consistent with the borrower's projected performance.

Some lenders originate ABL facilities with springing covenants, meaning the covenants are operable only when certain conditions defined in the loan agreements are not met. For example, cash dominion may not be required unless excess availability falls below an established threshold. A springing covenant arrangement is advantageous to the borrower as fewer restrictions provide more freedom to operate. Such arrangements can, however, adversely affect the controls that are the strength of an ABL credit. A bank that offers springing covenants should develop policies that establish clear guidelines outlining the appropriate use of such arrangements and effective risk mitigating requirements, which may include standards for the adequacy, stability, and preservation of liquidity.

The bank's loan policy should clearly establish financial covenant standards for ABL transactions. The lender should carefully review the borrower's information to determine the borrower's compliance. The bank should carefully analyze any violation to determine the root cause and appropriate corrective action. The decision to waive covenant requirements, at underwriting or subsequently during the life of the loan, should be documented and well supported. Failure to identify covenant violations or regularly waiving them may impair the lender's ability to enforce the covenants in the future.

## Pricing

ABL facilities are often priced based on a complex structure of fees and loan spreads that change based on performance. For example, the base for variable pricing may be the London InterBank Offered Rate (Libor), with the spread varying according to line availability and the borrower's financial leverage. Other pricing triggers may include delinquency, excess dilution rates, covenant violations, and over-advances. A loan agreement should clearly establish conditions that trigger interest rate changes, as well as fee-based servicing requirements. The fee structure typically includes customer charges for administrative costs, including field audits, lockbox arrangements, and appraisals.

Some banks may capitalize interest and fees by charging those costs to the ABL revolver instead of collecting payments in cash. The advantage to the bank is the ability to collect additional interest on those balances. While this practice is considered a sign of a borrower's financial weakness in most forms of commercial lending, it is a long-standing and normal practice in ABL and is not, by itself, cause for an adverse risk rating.

## Over-Advances

An over-advance can dilute the collateral coverage and may cause the lender to be under-collateralized, creating what is commonly referred to as a "stretch piece" or "airball."

Over-advances should be approved in accordance with the bank's loan policies and be supported by an assessment of the adequacy of the company's cash flow to repay the over-advance. Credit approval and loan documents should explicitly state when and under what conditions the lender permits an over-advance. The documents should stipulate the amount, frequency, duration, and period of the year when an over-advance is permitted. Over-advances in excess of prudent advance rates or that rely on cash flow for repayment weaken the ABL loan structure and should have a defined repayment plan with repayment over a short term. Most banks do not allow an over-advance in excess of 10 to 15 percent of the borrowing base. The bank should also make every effort to verify that the borrower is using the proceeds as designated rather than masking obsolete inventory or slow sales.

An unapproved over-advance in ABL may indicate a serious deficiency in the administration of the loan or inaccurate reporting by the borrower. The bank should immediately develop a strategic response that could include demanding repayment, renegotiating the terms of the loan, or even liquidation of collateral. Renegotiation affords the bank the opportunity to add collateral, guarantor support, or collateral controls.

# Third-Party Guarantees or Insurance

Third-party guarantees or insurance are common features associated with ABL facilities. Credit insurance, in particular, can be tailored to provide funds beyond the loan amount to cover items, such as accounts payable, that could affect the bank's lien status and ability to liquidate inventory. This can assure the bank's security interest in the collateral and protection as loss payee. Such a bank may also be able to justify increased advance rates and credit availability based on the reduced level of risk. The increased availability benefits the borrower and, in some cases, may offset the borrower's cost of obtaining the insurance. In general, a healthy borrower is less likely to agree to the added cost of credit insurance if it has the ability to secure financing elsewhere without it.

Credit insurance underwriting requires participation by the bank and the borrower. Most insurers review the borrower's financials, assess the management team, evaluate the borrower's customer base and relationships with suppliers, and review the draft loan agreement between the borrower and the bank. This process is central to determining insurance premium costs and can serve as a risk management check for the bank.

There are also government-sponsored programs that support foreign trade, such as the Export-Import Bank of the United States and the Foreign Credit Insurance Association.

# ABL Administration

The complexity of administering ABL loans results in higher transaction risk than for most other types of commercial loans. ABL departments should be structured with a distinct separation of administrative duties between employees responsible for credit approval, collateral/cash proceeds control, field audits, and portfolio management. Lending units that allow employees to perform conflicting roles can increase the bank's operational risk.

Prudent administration of an ABL loan is integral to controlling credit and operational risk. Loan agreements are typically complex, particularly with regard to collateral requirements, and ensuring compliance with administrative requirements is labor-intensive. To be successful, an ABL program must have an experienced and adequately staffed back-office operation. The examiner should evaluate whether employees are sufficiently trained and experienced to perform their responsibilities and should assess the quality of internal controls and audit systems. Because the overhead costs of properly administering ABL can be high, some banks may be tempted to cut costs in this area. An examiner reviewing a bank with smaller volumes of ABL loans should pay particular attention to the adequacy of staffing, controls, and monitoring systems.

ABL activities should be supported by strong management information systems (MIS) that can accurately compile and track information. Reports should be timely and accurate. Good MIS enables an ABL lender to identify over-advances and changes in borrowing patterns or collateral quality. Timely identification allows the bank to take swift action to control risks. The examiner should evaluate the bank's systems against the range of risks assumed.

When a borrower has loans with more than one unit of a bank, one of the units should be assigned primary responsibility for the entire relationship. This can make the relationship easier to monitor, help ensure that the borrower is treated consistently, and maximize the bank's recovery in the event of a troubled credit. Most often, because of the special requirements associated with ABL, the ABL unit is best suited to be the responsible unit.

An ABL borrower's financial condition may become more difficult to monitor when the borrower has credit relationships with other financial institutions. ABL facilities often include a covenant in the loan agreement that prevents borrowing at another institution without the original banks' knowledge and consent. Prudent banks specifically prohibit ABL facilities at other institutions because of the control issues associated with shared collateral. An ABL lender may not object to other types of borrowing, however, and may be comfortable with another lender providing specialized financing, equipment leasing, or a mortgage.

## Disbursing Revolving Loan Advances

An ABL lender can choose from many systems for controlling the disbursement of loan proceeds and monitoring collateral. The goal is to safeguard the bank if the borrower defaults; which process is best depends on the size of the bank's portfolio and the risk profile of the individual customer.

ABL units commonly exert strict control over the disbursement of loan proceeds. The most tightly controlled are fully followed lines, for which funds are advanced against specific supporting collateral documents (e.g., invoices, shipping documents, or receipts) that are verified and reconciled during field audits.

Some borrowers draw against the available borrowing base rather than against specific supporting collateral documentation. Because this type of revolving arrangement gives the bank less control over the loan proceeds, the bank should keep track of borrowing activity so that it can investigate any unusual activity. Borrowing patterns should conform closely to the buildup of inventory and collection of receipts as reported on the borrowing base certificates. Borrower-prepared cash flow projections should detail expected borrowing needs and repayment activity. An examiner should ascertain whether the bank exerts appropriate control over loan disbursements.

## Monitoring Systems

Effective monitoring and reporting systems are the foundation of prudent ABL risk management and should be achieved jointly between the borrower and the lender. The bank should investigate and develop a comprehensive understanding of the borrower's business, accounting practices, and reporting capabilities as part of the credit decision process. From there, the bank can determine the controls necessary to effectively monitor fluctuating collateral bases and the company's borrowing needs, as well as ensure that cash collateral proceeds are collected and appropriately applied to the loan balance.

## Monitoring the Borrowing Base

The most common collateral control in an ABL transaction is provided by a borrowing base arrangement. The borrowing base is the collateral base, agreed to by the borrower and lender, that limits the amount of funds the lender will advance to the borrower. The borrowing base specifies the maximum amount that can be borrowed in terms of collateral type, eligibility, and advance rates. The loan agreement establishes how the borrowing base is determined and how frequently it is recalculated.

The bank's biggest challenge when lending against a borrowing base is maintaining current and accurate information. An ABL borrower may be required to submit borrowing base certificates and supporting information (receivable agings, inventory reports, etc.) as frequently as daily, depending on the borrower's risk profile and the nature of the collateral. The certificates and supporting reports often serve as the bank's primary sources of information regarding changes in the borrower's financing needs, cash conversion cycle, and collateral condition. It is important, therefore, that the lender develops a sound understanding of the borrower's business and reporting systems and verifies the integrity of the borrower's reporting systems through regular field audits.

## Monitoring Receivables

Monitoring receivables is labor-intensive. Bank personnel need to verify borrower compliance with the loan agreement; identify trends in receivables quality, turnover rates, and concentrations; and update credit availability.

An ABL lender should require an aging of receivables that lists receivables by customer name, balance outstanding, and current payment status. Each day (or less frequently if the agreement so stipulates), the lender should adjust the maximum amount of credit available based on eligible receivables and cash receipts. The bank should review the borrowing base revisions and loans outstanding to make sure the borrower is conforming to limits. If the borrower is required to only certify compliance, the bank should have a system to ensure that compliance certifications are received by the due dates. The accuracy of compliance certification is reviewed during a field audit. A bank secured by blanket assignment of receivables needs to conduct timely reviews of financial information to determine the current level of collateral support.

## Monitoring Inventory

Inventory can become obsolete or build to excessive levels. Either situation adversely affects the marketability of the inventory, the financial condition of the borrower, and the collateral position of the bank.

The cause of excess inventory can be beyond the borrower's control (an economic downturn), within the borrower's control (an overly optimistic sales forecast), or a combination of both (failure by the borrower to react appropriately to competition from a new entity or product line). Inventory usually becomes obsolete when better products enter the marketplace. Although obsolescence risk can affect virtually any business, the risk is higher when the product life cycle is shorter, for example, in industries such as apparel and electronics.

A write-down of excess or obsolete inventory affects the borrower (lower profits) and the bank (lower collateral value). If a write-down is significant, and they frequently are, capital and liquidity can come under pressure and a revolver can become over-advanced. The banker and examiner should carefully analyze a borrower's switch from either first in, first out (FIFO) to last in, first out (LIFO) or from LIFO to FIFO inventory accounting, because these practices can conceal inventory and operating problems.

## Lockbox and Cash Dominion Arrangements

In most ABL transactions, the bank either controls or reserves the right to control the borrower's cash receipts. Lockbox arrangements, wherein the borrower's customers are directed to send payments to a post office box where payments are collected and applied to a collateral deposit account controlled by the bank, are an integral part of ABL. The bank may elect to exercise full dominion or springing dominion over the cash receipts. Under a full dominion arrangement, the bank controls the cash collections and applies the necessary proceeds to the borrower's loan account before releasing any funds. In a springing dominion arrangement, the bank collects and then transfers the cash receipts to the borrower's account, provided the borrower complies with the loan agreement. The borrower controls the application of the proceeds thereafter. A bank exercising springing dominion reserves the right to control and apply proceeds if the borrower fails to meet a loan requirement as specified in the loan agreement, such as an excess availability standard.

A lockbox arrangement benefits both parties. The bank gains the ability to monitor receivables and cash flows continuously while reducing the risk of borrower fraud. The borrower benefits by receiving credit more quickly for receivables payments, and the bank assumes some of the borrower's bookkeeping tasks.

## Lien Status Monitoring

A banker should ensure that collateral liens are properly perfected and maintained. For example, a banker overseeing ABL collateral needs a tickler system to alert the bank to file continuation statements for financing statements (UCC filings), which generally expire after five years. If the bank does not continue the statements, the lender's security interest is at risk. The bank should also conduct periodic lien searches, particularly for higher-risk borrowers. A lien search discloses any other party that has filed a security interest in collateral. It is especially important to uncover purchase money interests and tax liens, because they can take priority over the bank's lien.

## Fraud

Fraud is a frequent cause of loss in ABL. Regular collateral monitoring and timely field audits are the best deterrents to fraud-related losses. Because fraud can significantly reduce collateral values, a bank should make sure not to advance funds against nonexistent collateral. A fraudulent borrower can submit falsified sales and collection documentation, use the same receivables as collateral to obtain financing from more than one bank, divert cash or collateral proceeds, misrepresent purchase orders, or overstate inventory levels.

## Third-Party Vendors and Automation

Tracking, monitoring, and reporting ABL collateral can be a manual, time-intensive process prone to human error and fraud. Many banks find this type of monitoring difficult and have sustained losses as a result. The desire to streamline monitoring has given way to the increased popularity and use of automated monitoring systems. These systems can provide a number of benefits when properly implemented, including

- lower losses from credit risk and fraud, because the systems enhance the bank's ability to detect problems early and minimize the risk of borrower fraud.
- reduced administrative costs and more effective time management.
- a standardized approach to ABL risk management.

- a better relationship between bank and borrower, because the systems allow instant feedback, greater transparency, and more information that the borrower can use to improve the business.

Automated systems from third-party vendors link the borrower's financials with the bank. Most systems have the ability to analyze the financials against the bank's borrowing base formula and calculate the current borrowing availability. The borrower and bank receive reports detailing credit availability and borrowing base trends that help manage, monitor, and track receivables and inventory.

The OCC expects banks and their boards of directors to properly oversee and manage third-party relationships. Third-party risk management systems should reflect the complexity of third-party activities and the overall level of risk involved. For a discussion of third-party risk management, refer to OCC Bulletin 2013-29, "Third-Party Relationships: Risk Management Guidance."

## Purchasing Participations in ABL Transactions

A bank that participates in ABL through the purchase of loan participations is expected to perform the same analysis as though the bank had originated the loans. As outlined in OCC Banking Circular 181 (Rev), "Purchases of Loans in Whole or in Part-Participations," a bank purchasing loans and loan participations must make thorough, independent evaluations of the transactions and the risks involved before committing any funds. The bank should apply the same standards of prudence, credit assessment and approval criteria, and "in-house" limits that would be employed if the purchasing organization were originating the loan. At a minimum, standards for the following should be addressed in policies and procedures:

- Obtaining and independently analyzing full credit information before purchasing the participation and regularly thereafter.
- Obtaining from the lead lender copies of all executed and proposed loan documents, legal opinions, title insurance policies, UCC searches, and other relevant documents.
- Monitoring the borrower's performance throughout the life of the loan.
- Establishing appropriate risk management guidelines.

## Debtor-in-Possession Financing

DIP financing refers to a financing arrangement provided to a borrower operating as a debtor under Chapter 11 bankruptcy. A borrower that successfully petitions for Chapter 11 bankruptcy is afforded a stay of legal action from creditors to provide time to formulate and submit a plan of reorganization to the bankruptcy court. As part of the bankruptcy, the borrower retains control of its business assets and operations as a DIP.

DIP financing is often provided by the same bank that financed the company before the company filed its petition for bankruptcy. This commonly occurs because the special rules and procedures in bankruptcy can provide the bank with certain benefits and protections that are not available outside of bankruptcy, including protection of collateral values—by allowing the bankrupt business to continue as a going concern—and protection of the bank's lien.

A DIP loan is collateralized by specific assets and generally assumes priority in payments and collateral lien position over all other obligations of the debtor. This is known as a super-priority claim. When the DIP loan is solely to provide new funding, the collateral may be composed of unencumbered assets or assets acquired post-petition. A DIP facility also may replace, or be consolidated with, some pre-petition debt. In this case, collateral may include a combination of pre-petition and post-petition assets. A pre-petition lender that also provides the DIP facility may cross-collateralize loans, subject to court approval.

A DIP financing arrangement is often structured as an ABL revolver with a borrowing base commonly consisting of accounts receivable and inventory. The lender monitors the collateral and administers collections through a comprehensive control structure that includes frequent collateral reporting and borrower certifications along with periodic field audits of the borrower's financial records and physical inventory. Self-liquidation of the credit facility may be enabled through

- lender control and application of cash receipts through a cash dominion account.
- lender control of loan advances through a borrowing base formula that incorporates conservative advance rates, appropriate eligibility requirements for receivables and inventory, and availability sub-limits and reserves, when prudent.

The strict controls and monitoring provided by an ABL structure are central to DIP risk management, but the controls should not be used as a substitute for credit due diligence. The lender should seek the counsel of experienced bankruptcy attorneys before engaging in a DIP financing arrangement. A DIP lender needs to determine whether

- the borrower's reorganization plan is likely to be approved by the courts.
- additional borrowing beyond the DIP financing may be required.
- the lender is likely to receive repayment upon the court's confirmation of the reorganization plan.
- the plan protects the lender's collateral if the bankruptcy filing becomes a Chapter 7 liquidation case.
- the plan assigns priority lien status to the post-petition DIP financing.

Lenders also need to be aware of the following factors that can impair the pre-petition debt:

- Without post-petition financing, the company may be forced to liquidate. Forced liquidation may result in lower collateral proceeds and creditors will likely incur higher losses.
- Although a secured creditor may be deemed to be adequately protected under the plan, the company's use of the lender's collateral may diminish the value of those assets.
- Under certain conditions, the court may bestow a superior lien for DIP financing that enables the DIP lender to supersede the pre-petition lender's lien.

Ideally, if the borrower's reorganization plan is successful, the company should achieve sufficient financial stability to emerge from bankruptcy and resume operations as a going concern. Successful reorganization typically results in full repayment of DIP loans. An unsuccessful reorganization may result in the sale of the company or asset liquidation under which it is unlikely that all DIP debts would be fully satisfied.

## Credit Risk Rating Considerations

When risk rating ABL facilities, it is important to keep in mind that ABL is a collateral-focused type of commercial lending intended to prudently extend credit to borrowers that operate in highly seasonal industries or that may not qualify for traditional cash-flow-based loans. ABL revolving credit is extended based on the value and liquidity of the borrower's assets, the collateral control structure, and the bank's ability to monitor the assets. An examiner's analysis and risk-rating assessment of an ABL facility should focus on the following factors:

- The primary source of repayment for the facility.
- The quality and liquidity of the pledged collateral.
- The strength of the credit structure and controls.
- Actual performance versus planned performance at underwriting.
- The capital position and legal structure of the facility relative to repayment priority and the sharing of collateral proceeds.

Properly structured and fully followed ABL revolvers should be risk rated on a liquidity basis (as opposed to cash flow basis) when the following circumstances are present:

- Liquidity, including excess availability but exclusive of hard blocks, is sufficient to cover cash flow shortfalls and meet future liquidity needs over a reasonable period. Liquidity is usually considered sufficient if it can cover the borrower's actual cash burn over the last 12 months and the upcoming 12 to 18 months.
- Liquidity trends are reasonable, consistent with reliable projections, and unlikely to be affected by extraordinary liquidity needs.
- Operating performance is reasonable and does not pose a material threat to liquidity or turnaround potential, if applicable.
- The credit is self-liquidating in nature, with little or no reliance on illiquid borrowing base collateral or over-advances.
- The credit is stand-alone and not pari passu with other credit facilities.
- Performance reasonably tracks to a viable turnaround plan, if applicable.

A facility that is not properly structured and controlled, is pari passu with other debt facilities, or does not have sufficient balance sheet liquidity and excess borrowing base availability is more appropriately risk rated on an operating performance and cash flow basis.

An examiner must consider the quality of the underlying collateral and collateral trends when making an ABL risk rating assessment on a liquidity basis. Collateral quality issues, such as receivable concentrations (particularly when not properly analyzed by the bank), lengthening of the operating cycle, recurring inventory write-downs, and unaddressed adverse field examination results should be properly reflected in the assessment of credit risk.

A thorough analysis of the borrower's operating performance and operating cash flow is important in properly risk rating an ABL relationship. While it may be considered a secondary source of repayment for an ABL revolver, operating cash flow is generally the primary source of repayment for an ABL term loan or over-advance and the key determinant in assessing term loan risk. An evaluation of operating performance and cash flow is important when other weaknesses exist in an ABL revolver, such as weak underwriting or collateral controls, liberal advance rates, illiquid borrowing base assets, over-advances, infrequent asset appraisals and field exams, and low excess availability thresholds for springing cash dominion and springing covenant testing.

Capital and legal structures are key components of an ABL risk-rating assessment. A revolving ABL facility is sometimes originated as a part of a larger debt structure. An ABL revolver that is structured as a stand-alone, fully followed facility secured by a first lien on working capital assets with strong controls and a specific source of repayment may be risk rated independently from other debt in most cases. Where an ABL facility is structured as pari passu with other senior debt and shares in repayment priority and collateral proceeds, the facility may be risk rated similarly to other senior credit facilities.

The terms of first- and last-out revolving ABL facilities can vary considerably. While the conversion of assets rather than operating cash flow is generally viewed as the primary source of repayment for a last-out tranche, the particular terms, collateral, cash flow, and the company's capital structure are also important considerations in risk rating these facilities.

The following list provides some characteristics that deserve an examiner's attention and may warrant an adverse risk rating:

- Failure to meet earnings or liquidity projections.
- A significant unplanned increase in cash burn or a decline in revolver availability.
- Excessive leverage.
- Unexpected debt needs outside of the ABL revolver.
- Significant recurring losses.
- Frequent over-advances with unreasonable repayment structures.
- Failure to perform on a related debt.
- Failure to provide timely financial information, including collateral monitoring information.

An adverse rating may also be appropriate if the bank must liberalize advance rates or definitions of eligibility, including the addition of fixed assets to the borrowing base, to keep the loan within formula. If liquidation of collateral (e.g., a forced sale by the bank or borrower) is an ABL loan's most likely source of repayment, the loan would likely be classified as substandard at best.

Trends in the borrower's operating cycle and overall financial performance can signify credit or collateral quality deterioration that could lead to an adverse risk rating. The following are examples of factors the lender and the examiner should investigate as the factors occur:

- Slowing inventory turnover or accounts receivable collection.
- Recurring inventory write-downs.
- Prime inventory sell-offs that adversely alter the mix of inventory.
- Extended payables.
- An inventory buildup not supported by sales.
- An out of formula borrowing base.
- Adverse field examination or appraisal results.
- Increases in monthly cash burn and liquidity needs.
- An unstable or rapid decline in excess availability.
- An operating performance that deviates materially from planned performance.
- Borrower inability to provide reliable projections of liquidity and borrowing needs.

Additional guidance on risk rating ABL loans is provided in appendix B, which includes examples of adversely rated credits and rating rationale. The "Leveraged Lending" booklet of the *Comptroller's Handbook* provides risk-rating guidance for loans to highly leveraged borrowers, and OCC Bulletin 2013-9, "Guidance on Leveraged Lending," describes supervisory expectations.

A bank that relies on sponsor support as a secondary source of repayment should establish guidelines for evaluating the qualifications of the sponsor and implement a process to monitor a sponsor's financial condition on a regular basis. A bank may consider sponsor support in assigning a risk rating when the institution can document the sponsor's history of demonstrated support and its economic incentive, capacity, and stated intent to continue to support the transaction.

## Risk-Rating Considerations for DIP Loans

The OCC's approach to risk rating DIP loans is the same as with other types of commercial lending. The strengths and weaknesses of each DIP loan should be evaluated and risk-rating conclusions derived on a case-by-case basis. A DIP facility should not receive a pass rating if there is a material probability of default, even when the credit structure and collateral protection are strong. The borrower must have the ability to generate sufficient cash to service the DIP facilities, maintain trade relationships, and meet other needs, such as nondiscretionary capital expenditures.

The primary evaluation criteria are the strength of the repayment source and the probability of repayment. Key factors in assessing these criteria in DIP facilities are the quality and liquidity of the collateral position, loan structure, and loan controls. The DIP lender's priority lien status alone is not sufficient to mitigate the risk that typically exists with a DIP borrower. Additional controls are needed that create a self-liquidating structure for the facility. The central issue is often whether the strength of structural and collateral factors provides

adequate mitigation of the well-defined credit weaknesses generally present in a bankrupt borrower.

To adequately mitigate credit risk, a DIP loan should be secured by collateral that is of high quality and liquid. Factors to evaluate include receivable agings, customer concentrations and creditworthiness, inventory composition and marketability, borrowing base exclusions, and the degree of reliance on alternative assets. Conditions in the borrower's industry also affect collateral. Industry weakness may diminish the quality of receivables and inventory that will almost certainly have a significant effect on the value and marketability of fixed assets. Lastly, adherence to the borrowing base formula is a necessity. Over-advances represent a credit weakness that should mandate classification.

The probability of emergence from bankruptcy must also be assessed. This assessment requires the application of traditional credit analysis, with the primary focus on post-petition operating trends and results. This requires more than a plan. Reorganization typically includes substantial cost cutting, improved revenue generation, or both. A sale of noncore assets may also be necessary. Evidence of positive cash flow trends and reasonable expectations for a stable and adequate cash flow level to support emergence are critical to a satisfactory credit rating. Emergence from bankruptcy ultimately relies on obtaining exit financing, which depends on achieving a similar level of credit support.

In summary, a pass rating may be warranted for a DIP loan when the loan is soundly structured and the primary source of repayment is strong enough to repay the loan within that structure. Repayment chances are improved and credit risk is mitigated when the quality and liquidity of collateral, in conjunction with strong credit structure and controls, indicate that the loan is essentially self-liquidating and that the post-petition operations provide reasonable support that the borrower will emerge from the bankruptcy. If any of these factors are absent, the well-defined credit weaknesses are not adequately mitigated, and the DIP loan should be classified.

## Problem Loan Management

A bank should formulate an individual action plan with clear and quantifiable objectives and time frames for an adversely rated or otherwise high-risk borrower whose operating performance deviates significantly from planned asset conversion, collateral values, or other important targets. Actions may include working with the borrower for an orderly resolution while preserving the bank's interests, selling the loan in the secondary market, or liquidation. The examiner and the bank need to ensure that problem credits are reviewed regularly for risk-rating accuracy, accrual status, recognition of impairment through specific allocations, and charge-offs.

The bank should notify the borrower well in advance if the borrower's line of credit will be canceled—giving the borrower time to seek other sources of credit—or if receivables and inventory will be liquidated. In order to reduce the possibility of litigation, a lender should communicate regularly with a borrower when concerns arise and should document any decisions to take action. The lender must exercise caution when taking action against a customer and should consult legal counsel first. To prevent fraud, the lender may need to intensify collateral monitoring after such a notification. Comprehensive training programs for bank staff should include adequate training in lender liability and other compliance issues.

## Allowance for Loan and Lease Losses

A bank should ensure that its allowance for loan and lease losses (ALLL) methodology accurately reflects the bank's historical loss experience and other relevant factors. The OCC encourages banks to segment their loan portfolios into as many components as practical to provide a more thorough evaluation of expected loan losses. Bank management should segment a loan portfolio by first identifying risk characteristics that are common to a group of loans, such as ABL transactions. Consideration should be given to further segmentation of the ABL portfolio based on industry concentrations and other characteristics such as loan structure and controls. Refer to the "Allowance for Loan and Lease Losses" booklet of the *Comptroller's Handbook* for additional guidance.

# Examination Procedures

This booklet contains expanded procedures for examining specialized activities or specific products or services that warrant attention beyond the core assessment contained in the "Community Bank Supervision," "Large Bank Supervision," and "Federal Branches and Agencies Supervision" booklets of the *Comptroller's Handbook*. Examiners determine which expanded procedures to use, if any, during examination planning or after drawing preliminary conclusions during the core assessment.

## Scope

These procedures are designed to help examiners tailor the examination to each bank and determine the scope of the ABL examination. This determination should consider work performed by internal and external auditors and other independent risk control functions and by examiners in related areas. Examiners need to perform only those objectives and steps that are relevant to the scope of the examination as determined by the following objective. Seldom is every objective or step of the expanded procedures necessary.

**Objective:** To determine the scope of the examination of ABL and identify examination objectives and activities necessary to meet the needs of the supervisory strategy for the bank.

1. Review the following sources of information and note any previously identified ABL-related problems that require follow-up:

    - The supervisory strategy.
    - The examiner-in-charge's (EIC) scope memorandum.
    - The OCC's information system.
    - Previous reports of examination (ROE) and work papers.
    - Internal and external audit reports, including loan reviews, and work papers.
    - Bank management's responses to previous ROEs and audit reports.
    - Customer complaints and litigation.

2. Obtain the results of reports such as the Uniform Bank Performance Reports and Canary.

3. Obtain and review policies, procedures, and reports bank management uses to supervise ABL. Consider

    - specific ABL policies and risk management guidelines.
    - internal risk assessments.
    - portfolio strategies.
    - ABL profitability reports.
    - loan trial balance, past-due accounts, and nonaccruals for ABL.
    - risk-rating stratification and migration reports.
    - list of marginal pass-rated credits.

- problem loan reports for adversely rated ABL loans.
- concentration reports.
- exception reports.
- reports used to monitor borrowing base compliance.
- reports used to monitor loans with modified borrowing base formulas since the last examination.
- loans with over-advances.
- loans transferred to the ABL unit from other divisions of the bank.
- board or loan committee reports and minutes related to ABL.
- ABL loans for which terms have been modified by a reduction of the interest rate or other repayment requirement, by a deferral of interest or principal, or by other restructuring of payment terms.
- loans on which interest has been capitalized since the initial underwriting.
- ABL participations purchased or sold since the last examination.
- ABL Shared National Credits (SNC).
- information about the composition of the ABL unit, including the organizational chart, résumés of senior staff, and lending authorities.
- ABL loans to insiders of the bank or any affiliate of the bank.

4. Analyze the composition of the ABL portfolio and any material changes since the last examination. Consider

- the volume and source of portfolio growth.
- trends in watch, classified, past-due, nonaccrual, and nonperforming assets, as well as losses.
- actual portfolio performance versus planned performance and the risk implications.
- significant concentrations, including by geography, industry, borrower type, and product.
- the quality of portfolios acquired from other institutions.
- the level, composition, and trend of policy, underwriting, and documentation exceptions and the potential risk implications.
- critical third-party relationships.

5. Discuss with management the composition of the ABL portfolio, ABL strategies, and underwriting standards. Consider

- growth goals and potential sources of new loans.
- growth outside the current market area.
- new products, business lines, or customer types.
- the ABL staff's experience and ability to implement strategic initiatives.
- current and projected concentrations of ABL, as well as management's plans to manage concentrations.

- significant changes in ABL policies, procedures, underwriting, personnel, or control systems. Pay particular attention to changes in risk appetite, advance rates, collateral eligibility, over-advances, covenants, collateral reporting, and field audit requirements.
- local, regional, and national economic trends that could affect the ABL portfolio. Determine whether management has factored such data into projections of loan growth and quality.
- the extent of syndicated distribution and participation activities and any related policy or strategic changes. Assess the age, nature, and level of SNC pipeline exposure.
- observations from examiner review of bank reports, as well as reports generated by the OCC and other third parties.

6. For FSAs, determine whether the FSA is approaching the investment limit set forth in 12 USC 1464.

7. Based on an analysis of information obtained in the previous steps and with input from the EIC, determine the scope and objectives of the ABL examination.

8. Select from the following examination procedures the steps necessary to meet examination objectives and the supervisory strategy.

# Quantity of Risk

## Conclusion: The quantity of each associated risk is (low, moderate, or high).

The quantity of risk considers the level or volume of risk. Consider the "Quantity of Credit Risk Indicators" (appendix C), as appropriate.

**Objective:** To determine the quantity of credit risk associated with ABL.

1. Analyze the quantity of credit risk. Consider the products, markets, geographies, technologies, volumes, exposure levels, quality metrics, concentrations, third-party relationships, etc.

2. Assess the effects of external factors, including economic, industry, competitive, and market conditions.

3. Assess the effects of potential legislative, regulatory, accounting, and technological changes on ABL.

4. Obtain the loan trial balance and select a sample of loans to review. The sample should be consistent with the examination objectives, supervisory strategy, and OCC district-specific business plans. The sample should also be used to test changes in underwriting, including borrowing base changes, and loans with over-advances. Refer to the "Sampling Methodologies" booklet of the *Comptroller's Handbook* for guidance on sampling techniques. Consider

   - new large loans.
   - new loan types.
   - loans originated in new markets.
   - loans with over-advances or loans originated to finance over-advances.
   - out-of-formula loans.
   - loans with borrowing base modifications.
   - loans with significant collateral or underwriting exceptions.
   - loans at or above the legal lending limit.
   - loans to insiders of the bank or any bank affiliates.
   - special mention and classified loans.
   - SNCs.

5. Obtain credit files for all borrowers in the sample and document line sheets with sufficient information to determine the risk rating and the quality of underwriting. The examiner should complete a thorough financial analysis of each borrower. The analysis should address

   - the expected source of repayment.

- the quality of the collateral and collateral controls, including
  - the borrowing base collateral, including quality and liquidity.
  - the reasonableness of the borrowing base formula, including advance rates, eligibility standards, blocks, and reserves.
  - the frequency of borrowing base certificate submission and other collateral reporting requirements, e.g., receivables agings and inventory schedules.
  - trends in dilution (disputes, returns, and offsets).
  - debtor account concentrations and debtor financial strength.
  - the composition of inventory, including the presence of functional obsolescence.
- the borrower's liquidity profile, including
  - customer and supplier concentrations.
  - excess availability levels and trends.
  - cash burn levels, trends, and liquidity coverage.
  - projected liquidity and borrowing needs.
- the borrower's trade cycle, trends, and exposure to material adverse effects from economic or industry influences such as cyclical downturns and competition.
- the frequency and results of field examinations and audits, including
  - the frequency of accounts receivable verification audits.
  - the frequency of inventory and fixed asset appraisals.
  - material adverse findings.
- loan covenant requirements currently in effect, as well as springing covenants.
- cash dominion currently in effect, as well as the reasonableness of springing arrangements.
- compliance with the loan agreement, including covenants and borrowing base requirements.
- the level of credit risk posed by the borrower's management team, including changes in the quality or composition of personnel. Determine whether
  - officer memorandums adequately address the ongoing quality, integrity, and depth of the management team.
  - provisions in the credit agreement, or other steps taken by the lender, to protect the lender from any adverse consequences of a change in the borrower's management (e.g., life insurance policies on key executives payable to the bank or covenants allowing the lender to reassess the relationship in the event of the loss of a key executive).
- the adequacy of the borrower's insurance policies.
- support for the rating decision, including any key structural, collateral, or control issues.

6. Determine whether cash flow is sufficient to service debt when the expected source of repayment is operating cash flow. Consider

- the adequacy of cash flow to amortize the debt over a reasonable period.
- working capital needs and changes.
- discretionary and nondiscretionary capital expenditures, product development expenses, and payments to shareholders.

- the level of other fixed payments and maintenance expenses.

7. Analyze any secondary support provided by guarantors and endorsers. If the underlying financial condition of the borrower warrants concern, determine the guarantor's or endorser's capacity and willingness to repay the credit.

8. Review the completed line sheets and summarize the loan sample results. The examiner responsible for the ABL review should ensure that

   - recommended loan risk-rating downgrades are identified and appropriately documented.
   - a list is maintained of structurally weak loans.
   - lists are maintained of loans not supported by current or complete financial information and loans with collateral documentation deficiencies.
   - a summary is completed addressing whether policy, underwriting, pricing, and documentation exceptions are identified, reported, and approved. If not, determine the cause and discuss with management.

9. Loan write-ups should be completed as necessary. Comments for ABL facilities should discuss, where relevant,

   - liquidity and excess availability trends.
   - the borrower's actual and projected liquidity coverage of cash burn.
   - any projected extraordinary liquidity or borrowing needs.
   - material appraisal or field examination issues.
   - the credit structure, controls, and collateral protection.

10. Review recent loan reviews of ABL and any related audit reports. If there are any adverse trends in quantitative measures of risk or control weaknesses reported, comment on whether and by how much they may increase credit risk.

11. Using a list of nonaccrual loans, test loan accrual records to ensure that interest income is not being improperly recorded.

12. If the bank actively engages in loan participation purchases and sales,

   - test participation agreements to determine whether the parties share in the risks and contractual payments on a pro rata basis.
   - determine whether the books and records properly reflect the bank's asset or liability.
   - determine whether the bank exercises similar controls over loans serviced for others as for the bank's own loans.
   - investigate any loans or participations sold immediately before the examination to determine whether any were sold to avoid criticism during the examination.

13. If the bank has participations in loans that qualify as SNCs,

    - determine whether the credits were sampled or assigned a risk rating as part of the most recent SNC annual review. For each loan in the sample that is also an SNC, transcribe appropriate information to the line sheet. Grade the loan the same as was done at the SNC review; do not perform additional file work on SNC loans.
    - determine whether the bank, as lead or agent, exercises similar controls and procedures over syndications and participations sold as it exercises for the bank's own loan portfolio.
    - determine whether the bank, as a participant in a credit agented by another party, exercises similar controls over those participations purchased as it exercises for loans it has generated directly.

14. Evaluate the adequacy of the ALLL for the ABL portfolio.

15. Discuss the results of the loan sample with the EIC or loan portfolio manager and bank management.

**Objective:** To determine the quantity of operational risk associated with ABL.

1. Evaluate the level of operational risk in the bank's ABL portfolio. Consider

    - product delivery systems.
    - product complexity.
    - lien perfection procedures.
    - collateral monitoring procedures.

2. Review the volume and trend of losses in the ABL portfolio. Determine the cause of significant or increasing losses. Discuss with bank management losses resulting from failed internal processes, inadequate internal controls, employee misconduct, or borrower fraud. Determine whether appropriate corrective action has been implemented.

3. Assess the effectiveness of independent testing.

    - Review audits and loan reviews of the bank's ABL portfolio performed since the previous examination.
    - Determine whether the audits and reviews were performed by an independent party.
    - Determine whether control weaknesses and other material weaknesses were properly identified and reported.

4. Provide conclusions to the EIC regarding the effect of ABL activities on the bank's operational risk profile.

**Objective:** To determine the quantity of compliance risk associated with ABL.

1.  Evaluate the level of the bank's compliance with commercial lending laws, rules, and regulations. Refer to the "References" section of this booklet for a list of applicable laws and regulations.

    *   Review compliance audit results. If violations or noncompliance were noted, determine whether management took adequate corrective action.
    *   Test compliance as necessary.

2.  Review pending litigation against the bank. Determine whether any litigation resulted from violations of law, lender liability claims, or ABL debt liquidation practices.

3.  Discuss findings with the EIC and provide conclusions regarding the effect of ABL activities on the bank's compliance risk profile.

**Objective:** To determine the level of strategic risk associated with ABL.

1.  Evaluate strategic risk within the bank's ABL portfolio. Consider the following factors:

    *   The bank's ABL strategy and any planned changes.
    *   Management's record of decision making.
    *   Board oversight of strategic initiatives.
    *   The quality of the bank's ABL policies, underwriting standards, and risk management systems, and whether they are consistent with the bank's business strategy and the board's risk appetite.
    *   The staff's ability to implement ABL strategies without exposing the bank to unwarranted risk.
    *   The due diligence process for new products and services.

2.  Discuss findings with the EIC and provide conclusions regarding the effect of ABL on the bank's strategic risk profile.

**Objective:** To determine the level of reputation risk associated with ABL.

1.  Evaluate reputation risk within the bank's ABL portfolio. Consider the following factors:

    *   Management's ability to anticipate and respond to market or regulatory changes that could affect reputation risk.
    *   The quality of the bank's ABL policies, credit administration, and problem loan workout function.
    *   The adequacy of ABL controls and independent testing.
    *   The volume of ABL-related litigation.

2. Determine the volume of the bank's syndicated credit activity, if applicable. Review related policies and procedures for appropriateness, and assess management's ability to meet moral, legal, and fiduciary responsibilities without incurring unwarranted reputation risk.

3. If the bank engages in a significant volume of complex structured finance transactions, review and assess management's due diligence procedures, oversight, and internal controls. Consider the results of structured finance reviews by the OCC or other independent parties.

4. Discuss the findings with the EIC and provide conclusions regarding the effect of ABL on the bank's reputation risk profile.

# Quality of Risk Management

## Conclusion: The quality of risk management is (strong, satisfactory, or weak).

Determine the quality of risk management considering all risks associated with ABL lending. Consider the "Quality of Credit Risk Management Indicators" (appendix D of this booklet), as appropriate.

## Policies

Policies are statements of actions adopted by a bank to pursue certain objectives. Policies often set standards (on risk tolerances, for example) and should be consistent with the bank's underlying mission, values, and principles. A policy review should always be triggered when the bank's objectives or standards change.

**Objective:** To determine whether the board has adopted effective policies that are consistent with safe and sound banking practices and appropriate to the size, nature, and scope of the bank's ABL activities.

1. Evaluate relevant policies to determine whether they provide appropriate guidance for managing the bank's ABL function and are consistent with the bank's mission, values, and principles. Consider the impact of significant policy changes on the quantity of credit risk, if applicable. Policies and underwriting guidance should establish and detail the following:

   - Acceptable borrower types and industries.
   - Acceptable loan types and terms.
   - Credit analysis expectations regarding borrower, liquidity, and industry evaluations.
   - Collateral guidelines, including borrowing base components, advance rates on assets, and eligibility criteria.
   - Collateral monitoring requirements, including minimum standards for requiring, receiving, and verifying collateral reports and borrower certifications.
   - Expectations regarding the bank's control over cash and collateral proceeds, including the use of lockbox arrangements.
   - Minimum standards for collateral appraisals and field audits, including scope, timing, frequency, and follow-up.
   - Procedures that establish proper perfection and maintenance of collateral liens.
   - Minimum standards for requiring, receiving, and analyzing borrower financial information.
   - Procedures governing the use of covenants and springing covenants.
   - Standards for approving over-advances.
   - Procedures for the use of third-party systems to monitor borrowers.

- Standards for the use of third-party guarantees or insurance programs.
- Procedures for approving exceptions to policy and underwriting guidance and maintaining MIS to track exceptions.

2. Determine whether policies establish risk limits or positions and specify prudent actions to be taken if the limits are exceeded.

- If the bank's activities include syndication and loan participation activities, additional policy guidance should address these issues:

**Syndications**

- Procedures for defining, managing, and accounting for failed syndications.
- Identification of any sales made with recourse and procedures for fully reflecting the risk of any such sales.
- A process to ensure that purchasers and syndicate members are provided with timely, current financial information.
- A process to determine the portion of a transaction to be held in the bank's ABL portfolio and the portion and acceptable time frame to be held for sale.
- Limits on the length of time transactions can be held in the held for sale account and policies for handling items that exceed those limits.
- Prompt recognition of losses in market value for loans classified as held for sale.
- Limits on the aggregate volume of short-term (bridge) financings extended to facilitate syndications.
- Procedures and MIS to identify, control, and monitor syndication pipeline exposure.
- Procedural safeguards to prevent conflicts of interest for the bank and affiliated entities, including securities firms.

**Loan Participations Purchased**

- Obtaining and independently analyzing full credit information before the participation is purchased and on a timely basis thereafter.
- Obtaining from the lead lender copies of all executed and proposed loan documents, legal opinions, title insurance policies, UCC searches, and other relevant documents.
- Carefully monitoring the borrower's performance throughout the life of the loan.
- Establishing appropriate risk management guidelines.

3. Verify that the board of directors periodically reviews and approves the bank's ABL policies.

# Processes

Processes are the procedures, programs, and practices that impose order on a bank's pursuit of its objectives. Processes define how daily activities are carried out. Effective processes are consistent with the underlying policies and are governed by appropriate checks and balances (such as internal controls).

**Objective:** To determine whether the bank has processes in place to define how ABL activities are carried out.

1. Evaluate whether processes are effective, consistent with underlying policies, and effectively communicated to appropriate staff. Determine

   - whether the board of directors has clearly communicated objectives and risk limits for ABL to the bank's management and staff.
   - whether communication to key personnel within the bank's ABL unit is timely.

2. Determine whether appropriate internal controls are in place and functioning as designed. Complete the internal control questionnaire, if necessary, to make this determination.

3. Determine the quality of the bank's credit administration processes. Upon completing the review of the loan sample, provide assessments of

   - the appropriateness of the approval process and credit analysis.
   - the accuracy and integrity of the internal risk-rating process.
   - the volume, trend, and nature of loan policy and underwriting exceptions.
   - the timeliness of collateral valuations, borrower certifications, and financial statements.
   - the quality of collateral monitoring.
   - the effectiveness of lien perfection procedures.
   - loan covenant enforcement.

4. Evaluate the effectiveness of processes used to monitor collateral.

   - Determine how borrowing base certificates are reviewed for accuracy. Assess
     - the timeliness of receipt of supporting collateral reports, such as agings and inventory reports.
     - the frequency of reviews to ensure compliance with eligibility requirements.
     - the frequency of periodic audits.
     - the timeliness of identification of over-advances, including those created when delinquent receivables are eliminated.
   - Assess how inventory is monitored. Determine
     - the reasonableness of inventory valuation procedures.
     - the ability of the borrower's systems to identify stale or obsolete inventory and ensure it is removed from the borrowing base.
     - the frequency of inventory audits and appraisals.
   - Evaluate the effectiveness of the bank's process to verify the perfection of liens.
   - Determine whether proper control is maintained over cash and collateral proceeds.

- Assess the process to determine the accuracy of duplicate invoices. Determine whether duplicate invoices
  - are reviewed for eligibility under the borrowing base certificate.
  - are monitored for customer credit quality.
  - are removed from the borrowing base as soon as delinquency exceeds eligibility limits on past-due items.

# Personnel

Personnel are the bank staff and managers who execute or oversee processes. Personnel should be qualified and competent and should perform appropriately. They should understand the bank's mission, values, principles, policies, and processes. Banks should design compensation programs to attract, develop, and retain qualified personnel. In addition, compensation programs should be structured in a manner that encourages strong risk management practices.

**Objective:** To determine management's ability to supervise ABL in a safe and sound manner.

1. Given the scope and complexity of the bank's ABL activities, assess the management structure and staffing. Consider

   - the expertise, training, and number of staff members.
   - whether reporting lines encourage open communication and limit the chances of conflicts of interest.
   - the level of staff turnover.
   - specialized ABL training provided.
   - the use of outsourcing arrangements.
   - capability to address identified deficiencies.
   - responsiveness to regulatory, accounting, industry, and technological changes.

2. Assess performance management and compensation programs. Consider whether these programs measure and reward performance that aligns with the bank's strategic objectives and risk appetite.

   If the bank offers incentive compensation programs, determine whether they are consistent with OCC Bulletin 2010-24, "Interagency Guidance on Sound Incentive Compensation Policies," including compliance with the bulletin's three key principles: (1) provide employees with incentives that appropriately balance risk and reward, (2) be compatible with effective controls and risk management, and (3) be supported by strong corporate governance, including active and effective oversight by the bank's board of directors.

3. If the bank has third-party relationships that involve critical activities, determine whether oversight is consistent with OCC Bulletin 2013-29, "Third-Party Relationships: Risk Management Guidance."

# Control Systems

Control systems are the functions (such as internal and external audits, risk review, and quality assurance) and information systems that bank managers use to measure performance, make decisions about risk, and assess the effectiveness of processes. Control functions should have clear reporting lines, adequate resources, and appropriate authority. MIS should provide timely, accurate, and relevant feedback.

**Objective:** To determine whether the bank has systems in place to provide accurate and timely assessments of the risks associated with the bank's ABL activities.

1.  Evaluate the effectiveness of monitoring systems to identify, measure, and track exceptions to policies and established limits.

2.  Determine whether MIS provides timely, accurate, and useful information to evaluate risk levels and trends in the bank's ABL portfolio.

3.  Assess the scope, frequency, effectiveness, and independence of the internal and external audits of ABL activities. Consider the qualifications of audit personnel and evaluate accessibility to necessary information and the board of directors. Provide conclusions for

    -  the effectiveness of the bank's process to periodically evaluate internal controls. If the process is ineffective, examiners may need to perform additional testing.
    -  the effectiveness of independent testing of the accuracy and integrity of ABL data.
    -  the effectiveness of the bank's processes to ensure compliance with applicable laws, rulings, regulations, and accounting guidelines.
    -  the bank's process to remediate control deficiencies as well as other items noted in the external auditor's Schedule of Unadjusted Audit Differences or any other required communications provided by the external auditor. Items noted by the external auditor may indicate that additional testing should be performed by the examiners.

4.  Assess the effectiveness of the loan review function for ABL. Evaluate the scope, frequency, effectiveness, and independence of loan review, as well as the function's ability to identify and report emerging problems. Determine whether loan review reports address

    -  the quality of the ABL portfolio.
    -  the trend in portfolio quality.
    -  the quality of significant relationships.
    -  the level and trend of policy, underwriting, and pricing exceptions.

5. Assess the effectiveness of field audits for individual ABL borrowers. Evaluate the scope, timing, and frequency of the audits and the qualifications of the party performing the audits. Determine whether reports include

- an analysis of trends in accounts receivable, inventory, and accounts payable turnover.
- an analysis of trends in sales, returns, allowances, and discounts.
- the results of financial accounting record and control testing.
- verification of collateral.
- assessments of risk and potential compliance issues.

# Conclusions

## Conclusion: The aggregate level of each associated risk is (low, moderate, or high).
## The direction of each associated risk is (increasing, stable, or decreasing).

**Objective:** To determine, document, and communicate overall findings and conclusions regarding the examination of ABL.

1. Determine preliminary examination findings and conclusions and discuss with the EIC, including

   - the quantity of associated risks.
   - the quality of risk management.
   - the aggregate level and direction of associated risks.
   - the overall risk in ABL.
   - the frequency of future ABL examinations.
   - violations and other concerns.

   Use the following chart to document risk assessment ratings.

| Summary of Risks Associated With ABL | | | | |
|---|---|---|---|---|
| Risk category | Quantity of risk (Low, moderate, high) | Quality of risk management (Weak, satisfactory, strong) | Aggregate level of risk (Low, moderate, high) | Direction of risk (Increasing, stable, decreasing) |
| Credit | | | | |
| Operational | | | | |
| Compliance | | | | |
| Strategic | | | | |
| Reputation | | | | |

2. If substantive safety and soundness concerns remain unresolved that may have a material adverse effect on the bank, further expand the scope of the examination by completing verification procedures.

3. Discuss with bank management the examination findings, including violations, recommendations, and conclusions about risks and risk management practices. If necessary, obtain commitments for corrective action.

4. Compose conclusion comments, highlighting any issues that should be included in the ROE. Conclusion comments should address

   - the asset quality of the ABL portfolio.
   - the extent to which ABL credit risk and ABL credit risk management affect the risk profile of the bank.
   - the adequacy of policies and underwriting standards.
   - the volume and severity of underwriting and policy exceptions.
   - the quality of underwriting observed in the loan sample.
   - the reliability of internal risk ratings.
   - the quality of portfolio supervision and ABL staff.
   - the appropriateness of strategic plans.
   - the adequacy and timeliness of MIS.
   - the effectiveness of internal controls.
   - concentrations of credit.
   - compliance with applicable laws, rules, and regulations.

5. Update the OCC's information system and any applicable ROE schedules or tables.

6. Write a memorandum specifically setting out what the OCC should do in the future to effectively supervise ABL in the bank, including review periods, staffing, and workdays required.

7. Update, organize, and reference work papers in accordance with OCC policy.

8. Ensure any paper or electronic media that contain sensitive bank or customer information are appropriately disposed of or secured.

# Internal Control Questionnaire

An internal control questionnaire (ICQ) helps an examiner assess a bank's internal controls for an area. ICQs typically address standard controls that provide day-to-day protection of bank assets and financial records. The examiner decides the extent to which it is necessary to complete or update ICQs during examination planning or after reviewing the findings and conclusions of the core assessment.

## Policies

1. Has the board of directors, consistent with its duties and responsibilities, adopted written ABL policies that

    - establish procedures for reviewing ABL applications?
    - establish standards for ABL revolvers?
    - define acceptable collateral types and eligibility standards?
    - establish standards for collateral advance rates?
    - establish minimum requirements for initial and ongoing collateral verification?
    - establish minimum standards for loan and collateral documentation?

2. Are ABL policies reviewed at least annually to determine whether they are compatible with changing market conditions?

## Records

3. Is the preparation and posting of subsidiary ABL records performed or reviewed by employees who do not also

    - issue official checks and drafts?
    - handle cash?

4. Are the subsidiary ABL records reconciled at least monthly to the appropriate general ledger accounts, and reconciling items investigated by employees who do not also handle cash?

5. Are loan statements, delinquent account collection requests, and past-due notices checked to the trial balances that are used in reconciling subsidiary records with general ledger accounts, and handled only by employees who do not also handle cash?

6. Are inquiries about ABL loan balances received and investigated by employees who do not also handle cash?

7. Are documents supporting recorded credit adjustments to loan accounts or accrued interest receivable accounts checked or tested subsequently by employees who do not also handle cash? (If not, explain briefly.)

## Ledgering Accounts Receivable

8. Are terms, dates, weights, descriptions of merchandise, etc. that are shown on invoices, shipping documents, delivery receipts, and bills of lading scrutinized for differences?

9. Are procedures in effect to determine whether the signatures shown on the above documents are authentic?

10. Are payments from customers scrutinized for differences in invoice dates, numbers, terms, etc.?

## Loan Interest

11. Is the preparation and posting of loan interest records performed or reviewed by employees who do not also

   - issue official checks and drafts?
   - handle cash?

12. Are independent interest computations made and compared or tested to initial loan interest records by employees who do not also

   - issue official checks and drafts?
   - handle cash?

## Collateral

13. Does the bank record on a timely basis a first lien on the collateral for each borrower?

14. Does the bank maintain a system to verify lien perfection and monitor lien expirations on a regular basis?

15. Does the bank require independent collateral appraisals as part of the underwriting process?

16. Does the bank's ABL policy establish standards for reappraisals, including appraisal quality and frequency?

17. Does the bank verify the borrower's accounts receivable and inventory or require an independent verification on a periodic basis?

18. Does the bank require the borrower to provide agings, inventory schedules, and certifications on a periodic basis?

19. If applicable, are cash receipts and invoices block proved in the mailroom and subsequently traced to posting on daily transaction records?

20. Are those employees responsible for receiving and releasing collateral prohibited from making entries to the collateral register?

21. If applicable, is negotiable collateral held under joint custody?

## Conclusion

22. Is the foregoing information an adequate basis for evaluating internal controls, in that there are no significant additional internal auditing procedures, accounting controls, administrative controls, or other circumstances that impair any controls or mitigate any weaknesses indicated above? Explain negative answers briefly, and indicate conclusions as to their effect on specific examination or verification procedures.

23. Based on the answers to the foregoing questions, internal control for ABL is considered (strong, satisfactory, or weak).

# Verification Procedures

Verification procedures are used to verify the existence of assets and liabilities, or test the reliability of financial records. Examiners generally do not perform verification procedures as part of a typical examination. Rather, verification procedures are performed when substantive safety and soundness concerns are identified that are not mitigated by the bank's risk management systems and internal controls.

1. Test the additions of the trial balances and the reconciliations of the trial balances to the general ledger. Include loan commitments and other contingent liabilities.

2. Using an appropriate sampling technique, select loans from the trial balance and consider performing the following procedures:

   - Prepare and mail confirmation forms to borrowers. (Loans serviced by other institutions, either whole loans or participations, are usually confirmed only with the servicing institution. Loans serviced for other institutions, either whole loans or participations, should be confirmed with the buying institution and the borrower. Confirmation forms should include the borrower's name, loan number, original amount, interest rate, current loan balance, borrowing base, and a brief description of the collateral.)
   - After a reasonable time, mail second requests.
   - Follow up on any unanswered requests for verification or exceptions and resolve differences.
   - Examine notes for completeness and compare date, amount, and terms with the trial balance.
   - Check that disbursements are approved as required by the bank's procedures.
   - Check that the note is signed, appears to be genuine, and is negotiable.
   - Compare the description of the collateral held in ABL loan files with the description on the collateral register.
   - Determine whether the proper collateral documentation is on file.
   - Determine whether margins are reasonable and in line with bank policy and legal requirements.
   - Reconcile accounts receivable schedules and customer remittances to the lockbox account statements to ensure that all payments are being made to the account as required.
   - List all collateral discrepancies and investigate.
   - Obtain confirmation of any collateral held outside the bank (e.g., by bonded warehouses).
   - Determine whether each file contains documentation supporting guarantees and subordination agreements, when appropriate.
   - Determine whether any required insurance coverage is adequate and that the bank is named as loss payee.

- Review participation agreements, excerpting when necessary such items as rate of service fee, interest rate, retention of late charges, and remittance requirements, and determine whether participant has complied. Review disbursement ledgers and authorizations, and determine whether authorizations are signed in accordance with the terms of the loan agreement.

3. Review field audits and

   - determine whether on-site inspections are performed in conformance with bank policy.
   - consider making a physical inspection of the collateral when the quality or frequency of the bank's inspections is not adequate or if independence is in question.
   - if physical inspections are made, compare the results with the bank's records and investigate differences to the extent necessary.
   - reconcile differences with the results of the field audit and borrower provided information including borrowing base certificates.

4. Review appraisals and ensure they were ordered and conducted by competent and independent parties.

5. Review accounts with accrued interest by

   - reviewing and testing procedures for accounting for accrued interest and for handling adjustments.
   - scanning accrued interest for any unusual entries and following up on any unusual items by tracing them to initial and supporting records.

6. Using a list of nonaccrual loans, check loan accrual records to confirm that interest income is not being recorded.

7. Obtain or prepare a schedule showing the monthly interest income amounts and the commercial loan balance at the end of each month since the last examination and

   - calculate yield.
   - investigate any significant fluctuations or trends.

# Appendixes

## Appendix A: Trade Cycle Analysis Worksheet

The following worksheet can be used to express a company's trade cycle and working investment needs in days. The worksheet is useful for analyzing seasonal operating cycles and credits that are expected to repay at the end of the cycle. ABL loans that involve ongoing borrowings and companies with multiple operating cycles require more complex analyses to fully understand cash conversion and cash needs. The following analysis is most beneficial when performed at the low point of the operating cycle.

| Trade cycle analysis | Days[a] |
|---|---|
| Receivables/sales per day[b] | |
| + Inventory/sales per day | |
| **= Operating cycle** | |
| Less accounts payable/sales per day | |
| Less accruals/sales per day | |
| Less working capital/sales per day | |
| **= Net days[c]** | |
| | |
| Net days (if positive) | |
| x Sales per day | |
| **= Additional working capital** | |

[a] Per day calculations generally use 365 but may vary.

[b] Sales per day = ($ sales/days).

[c] If net days is negative, the borrower has sufficient working capital to clean up cyclical borrowings. If net days is positive, the borrower lacks sufficient working capital to clean up cyclical borrowings. To determine the amount of additional working capital needed to support the operating cycle, multiply net days times sales per day. The result is the approximate working capital shortfall.

# Appendix B: Risk-Rating Examples

## Example A: ABL Revolver

| Borrower | B & A Retail Inc. |
|---|---|
| Business | General merchandise and pharmaceutical products |
| Credit facility | $150 million four-year ABL revolver originated February 9, 20X0. The current outstanding balance is $90 million. |
| Pricing | Libor + 300 basis points |
| Repayment sources | Primary: Conversion of current assets to cash<br>Secondary: Refinancing<br>Tertiary: Collateral liquidation |
| Covenants and controls | The following covenants will spring into effect if excess borrowing availability falls below the $32 million soft block:<br><br>(1) Minimum earnings before deduction for interest, taxes, depreciation, and amortization (EBITDA) of 90 percent of projections<br>(2) Quarterly field examinations, semiannual collateral appraisals, and cash dominion<br><br>The loan agreement also limits maximum capital expenditures to $6.5 million in 20X2 and $10 million in 20X3. |
| Collateral | The revolver is secured by accounts receivable, inventory, and pharmacy scripts. Borrowing base availability governed by advance rates of 85 percent of eligible accounts receivable and 80 percent of the NOLV of inventory. Availability blocks of $32 million (soft) and $15 million (hard).<br><br>Borrowing base reports are provided weekly. The bank engaged a third-party appraisal valuation in the most recent quarter. The appraisal supported the borrowing base and did not result in any significant issues. |
| Financial synopsis | • The current borrowing base is $136 million with excess borrowing availability of $45 million, net of the hard block.<br><br>• The company experienced losses in 20X1 and 20X2 due to significant costs associated with discontinued operations, heavy capital expenditures associated with new stores, and the slow economy.<br><br>• New stores have started to produce results with year-to-date performance (three months) for 20X3 is consistent with plan. The company projects a net loss of $20 million in 20X3, much of which was recognized in 1QX3 as the company incurred additional costs associated with closing stores. Revenue is projected to improve as the company enters the peak selling season. No additional store closings or extraordinary expenses are projected.<br><br>• Cash burn is currently $2 million per month. The borrower projects no significant liquidity needs over the next 12 months. |
| Risk-rating decision | Pass<br>• Satisfactory liquidity<br>• Reasonable controls and structure<br>• Good collateral value supported by independent appraisal, current outstandings represent 66 percent of the margined borrowing base. |
| Rating discussion | The credit is rated pass based on a satisfactory and stable liquidity profile, reasonable control structure, and good collateral value. The soft block is reasonable and represents 21 percent of the revolver commitment. Current excess borrowing availability is sufficient to cover cash burn for the next 23 months, with no significant liquidity needs expected. |

| Alternate scenario | |
|---|---|
| **New information** | • Sales continue to deteriorate as the company has problems bringing new stores online. The borrower projects net losses in excess of $40 million in 20X3. Expected cash burn is $3 million per month.<br><br>• The borrowing base is $111 million with excess borrowing availability of $21 million (tripping the soft block). The borrower is working with consultants to develop a new business plan. Sale of the company or additional store closings are possible. |
| **Risk-rating decision** | Substandard/accrual<br><br>• Liquidity is not sufficient to fund cash burn beyond seven months.<br><br>• Operational performance and liquidity are expected to continue to deteriorate.<br><br>• Collateral coverage is adequate. |
| **Rating discussion** | Substandard due to well-defined weaknesses that include sustained poor operating performance and poor liquidity with negative cash flow that is continuing to deteriorate. Outstandings represent 81 percent of margined collateral. |

## Example B: ABL Revolver and Term Note

| Borrower | RPA Communications Inc. |
|---|---|
| Business | Communication systems integration |
| Credit facilities | (1) $435 million five-year revolver. Line originated October 15, 20X0. Maturity is scheduled for October 15, 20X5. Current outstanding balance is $100 million. Advances are governed by monthly borrowing base certificate. Terms also require a quarterly independent field audit.<br>(2) $2 billion 7-year term note originated on October 15, 20X0. Quarterly payments of interest plus quarterly principal amortization of 0.25 percent of the original loan amount. Balloon at maturity on October 15, 20X7. |
| Pricing | Libor + 325 basis points |
| Repayment sources | (1) Primary: Conversion of working assets to cash<br>Secondary: Refinancing<br>Tertiary: Collateral liquidation<br>(2) Primary: Operating cash flow<br>Secondary: Collateral liquidation |
| Covenants and controls | (1) Springing cash dominion if excess availability declines below $120 million for five consecutive days.<br>(2) Minimum fixed charge coverage ratio of 1.0x if availability declines below $120 million, tested quarterly. |
| Collateral | (1) First lien on working capital assets, primarily accounts receivable, second lien on all business assets. Eligible (< 90 days) accounts receivable (85 percent advance rate) and eligible inventory (60 percent of NOLV), consisting largely of readily valued and marketable generic components.<br>(2) First lien on all business assets, second-lien on borrowing base assets. Plant and equipment appraised at $2.5 billion (80 percent). |
| Financial synopsis | • The company has not fully achieved the expected synergies from the October 20X0 business acquisition but is within 5 percent of projections as of YE 20X2.<br>• Cash flow is not adequate to meet fixed charges despite the liberal amortization of the term note. The company generated fixed charge coverage ratios of 0.90x in 20X1 and 20X2.<br>• Since the beginning of 20X1, the company has been burning cash at a rate of $17 million per month. To date, the borrower has funded the cash burn with cash reserves. Current cash reserves total $20 million. Excess borrowing availability is $280 million. No extraordinary liquidity needs are expected in 20X3.<br>• Total debt to EBITDA leverage ratio is high at 4.80x.<br>• A field examination of the ABL collateral was performed in most recent quarter and identified no significant issues. Recent evaluation of plant and equipment shows no deterioration in value. |
| Risk-rating decision | (1) ABL revolver: Pass<br>• Adequate liquidity<br>• Adequate controls<br>(2) Term note: Substandard/Accrual<br>• Inadequate cash flow from operations<br>• High leverage<br>• Weak loan structure/repayment<br>• Adequate collateral margin |

| Rating discussion | (1) Liquidity is sufficient, availability of $280 million plus current cash reserves are sufficient to cover cash burn for 18 months. Controls are reasonable with availability covenants springing at 28 percent of commitment. The results of quarterly field audits have been satisfactory and collateral is reasonably liquid and fairly valued. Outstandings represent 26 percent of margined collateral.<br>(2) The term loan is risk rated substandard due to negative operating cash flow, high leverage, and a weak loan structure evidenced by negligible amortization. Accrual accounting treatment is supported by the collateral coverage. |
|---|---|
| **Alternate scenario** | |
| New information | • Sales and operating income declined in fiscal year 20X0 and fiscal year 20X1 as the company failed to effectively integrate its operations with the acquired business and has lost market share. Monthly cash burn is $25 million and cash reserves have been depleted. Fixed charge coverage ratio is .76x and breakeven is now expected to occur one year later than originally projected.<br>• Extended repayment terms have increased over 90-day receivables and credit memos for unsatisfied customers have increased. Erosion of the borrowing base has significantly reduced availability.<br>• Borrowing base is $280 million with $100 million outstanding and excess availability of $180 million available. |
| Risk-rating decision | (1) ABL revolver: Substandard/accrual<br>• Inadequate liquidity<br>• Results short of plan<br>• Adequate collateral coverage.<br>(2) Term note: Substandard/accrual<br>• Inadequate cash flow from operations<br>• High leverage<br>• Weak loan structure/repayment<br>• Adequate collateral coverage. |
| Rating discussion | (1) The ABL facility is rated substandard due to insufficient liquidity to cover anticipated cash burn for a reasonable period and financial performance that is short of plan. Reduction in availability and negative cash flow have reduced liquidity such that it covers projected cash burn for seven months.<br>(2) The term loan is substandard due to negative operating cash flow, high leverage, and a weak loan structure evidenced by negligible amortization. Accrual accounting treatment is supported by the collateral coverage. |

## Example C: DIP Financing

| Borrower | ABC Materials Corp. |
|---|---|
| Business | Steel stamping and fabrication |
| Credit facility | $70 million new money ABL DIP facility, 36-month tenor maturing May 14, 20X3. Full cash dominion in effect as well as daily reporting on receivables and inventory and a 13-week rolling cash flow. Borrowing base certificates are not required. Current outstanding balance is $45 million. |
| Pricing | 30-day Libor + 300 basis points |
| Repayment sources | Primary: Conversion of working assets as going concern<br>Secondary: Liquidation of collateral |
| Guaranty | None |
| Covenants and controls | Minimum performance of 90 percent of projected sales/cash receipts, tested quarterly. Fixed charge coverage ratio of 1.0x beginning in month 12, increasing to 1.15x in month 24, tested quarterly. Full cash dominion, daily reporting, quarterly field audits. |
| Collateral | First lien on inventory, receivables and cash, second lien on all other business assets. As of May 10, 20X1, the value of the first-lien collateral was $77 million. The collateral breakdown was as follows:<br><br>• Cash of $2 million<br>• Accounts receivable of $30 million<br>• Inventory of $45 million<br><br>DIP advances are governed by the following borrowing base factors:<br><br>• 80 percent advance rate on eligible receivables<br>• 85 percent of the NOLV of inventory ($55 million cap)<br>• Availability block of $750,000 for professional fees<br><br>As of May 10, 20X1, the borrowing base was $62 million. Collateral securing the second lien provides little support. |
| Financial synopsis | • The company filed for Chapter 11 bankruptcy on May 14, 20X1 after an abrupt deterioration in operating performance and liquidity tied directly to adverse market conditions. Excess availability at the time of filing was $8 million as compared with a monthly cash burn of $1 million. Although cash burn had stabilized, projected liquidity would have been enough to carry the company for only eight months.<br><br>• The company maintained a selective credit policy resulting in acceptable quality receivables despite a difficult market for its customers. Eligible inventory consists of raw materials and finished goods that are readily marketable. Field audits have been satisfactory.<br><br>• Management devised a credible plan to restructure its operations which, along with noncore asset sales and an already improving operating environment, would allow it to achieve breakeven in 12 months and return to full profitability by month 24 according to well supported projections. Excess availability is $26 million. |
| Risk-rating decision | Pass<br>• Adequate liquidity<br>• Adequate structure and controls |
| Rating discussion | Well-supported projections show liquidity could carry the company over the next 27 months given cash burn at $1 million. Collateral and advance rates are reasonable and controls are appropriate. There is a good likelihood that the company will emerge from bankruptcy prior to maturity. |

| Alternate scenario | |
|---|---|
| **New information** | • Before filing, the borrower experienced a sharp decline in revenues over the preceding 18 months. The borrower's bankruptcy plan indicates that although significant cost reduction measures have been instituted by the company, significant cash burn and losses are expected to continue.<br><br>• The existing lender provided a $62 million post-petition facility with a tenor of six months. Post-petition availability is $18.25 million with monthly cash burn of $2.5 million.<br><br>• Primary source of repayment is the sale of the company, either in part or whole.<br><br>• The investment banker retained by the company has identified a buyer for the company. The purchaser has provided a letter of intent to purchase the company within 60 days. The purchase price is $100 million and is subject to final due diligence and securing third-party financing. |
| **Risk-rating decision** | Substandard/accrual<br><br>• Insufficient liquidity<br><br>• Poor operating performance<br><br>• Company is unlikely to successfully emerge from bankruptcy<br><br>• Controls are satisfactory<br><br>• Collateral coverage is satisfactory |
| **Risk-rating discussion** | Post-petition liquidity is weak with excess availability sufficient to cover only eight months of cash burn. Poor operating performance is projected to continue for at least the next 12 to 18 months. Company is unlikely to successfully emerge from bankruptcy with company sale or liquidation now the most likely source of repayment. Pending sale is contingent on due diligence and financing. ABL controls, including full cash dominion and daily reporting, are satisfactory. Collateral coverage is satisfactory with outstandings representing 72 percent of borrowing base. |

# Appendix C: Quantity of Credit Risk Indicators

Examiners should consider the following indicators when assessing the quantity of credit risk associated with ABL activities.

| Low | Moderate | High |
|---|---|---|
| The level of ABL loans outstanding is low relative to capital. | The level of ABL loans outstanding is moderate relative to capital. | The level of ABL loans outstanding is high relative to capital. |
| ABL growth rates are supported by local, regional, or national economic trends. Growth, including off-balance-sheet activities, has been planned for and is commensurate with management and staff expertise and operational capabilities. | ABL growth rates exceed local, regional, or national economic trends. Growth, including off-balance-sheet activities, has not been planned for or exceeds planned levels and may test the capabilities of management, ABL staff, and MIS. | ABL growth rates significantly exceed local, regional, or national economic trends. Growth has not been planned for or exceeds planned levels, and stretches the experience and capability of management, ABL staff, and MIS. Growth may also be in new products or outside the bank's traditional lending area. |
| Interest and fee income from ABL activities is not a significant portion of loan income. | Interest and fee income from ABL activities is an important component of loan income; however, the bank's lending activities remain diversified. | The bank is highly dependent on interest and fees from ABL activities. Management may seek higher returns through higher-risk product or customer types. Loan yields may be disproportionate relative to risk. |
| The bank's ABL portfolio is well diversified, with no single large concentrations or a few moderate concentrations. Concentrations are well within reasonable risk limits. The ABL portfolio mix does not materially affect the risk profile. | The bank has a few material ABL concentrations that may approach internal limits. The ABL portfolio mix may increase the bank's credit risk profile. | The bank has large ABL concentrations that may exceed internal limits. The ABL portfolio mix increases the bank's credit risk profile. |
| ABL underwriting is conservative. ABL loans with structural weaknesses or underwriting exceptions are occasionally originated; however, the weaknesses are effectively mitigated. | ABL underwriting is satisfactory. The bank has an average level of ABL loans with structural weaknesses or exceptions to underwriting standards. Exceptions are reasonably mitigated and consistent with competitive pressures and reasonable growth objectives. | ABL underwriting is liberal and policies are inadequate. The bank has a high level of ABL loans with structural weaknesses or material underwriting exceptions. The volume of exceptions exposes the bank to increased loss in the event of default. |
| Collateral requirements and advance rates are conservative. Collateral controls and monitoring are effective. Collateral valuations are reasonable, timely, and well supported. Field audits are timely and appropriate. | Collateral requirements are acceptable. Advance rates are moderate, but mitigated by satisfactory controls and monitoring systems. Some collateral valuations may not be well supported or timely. Field audits are generally appropriate. | Collateral requirements are liberal. Advance rates may be aggressive. Collateral controls and monitoring systems may not effectively mitigate risk. Collateral valuations are not regularly obtained, frequently unsupported, or reflect inadequate protection. Field audits are inadequate or not performed in a timely manner. |

| Low | Moderate | High |
|---|---|---|
| ABL loan documentation or collateral exceptions are low and have minimal impact on the bank's risk profile. | The level of ABL loan documentation or collateral exceptions is moderate; however, exceptions are reasonably mitigated and corrected in a timely manner. The risk of loss from these exceptions is not material. | The level of ABL loan documentation or collateral exceptions is high. Exceptions are not mitigated or not corrected in a timely manner. The risk of loss from the exceptions is heightened. |
| ABL loan distribution across the pass category is consistent with a conservative risk appetite. Migration trends within the pass category favor the less risky ratings. Lagging indicators, including past dues and nonaccruals, are low and stable. | ABL distribution across the pass category is consistent with a moderate risk appetite. Migration trends within the pass category may favor riskier ratings. Lagging indicators, including past dues and nonaccruals, are moderate and may be slightly increasing. | ABL distribution across the pass category is heavily skewed toward riskier pass ratings. Lagging indicators, including past dues and nonaccruals, are moderate or high and the trend is increasing. |
| The volume of adversely rated ABL loans is low and is not skewed toward more severe risk ratings. | The volume of adversely rated ABL loans is moderate, but is not skewed toward more severe ratings. | The volume of adversely rated ABL loans is moderate or high, skewed to the more severe ratings, and increasing. |
| ABL refinancing and renewal practices raise little or no concern regarding the quality of ABL loans and the accuracy of problem loan data. | ABL refinancing and renewal practices pose some concern regarding the quality of ABL loans and the accuracy of problem loan data. | ABL refinancing and renewal practices raise substantial concerns regarding the quality of ABL loans and the accuracy of problem loan data. |

# Appendix D: Quality of Credit Risk Management Indicators

Examiners should consider the following indicators when assessing the quality of credit risk management for ABL activities.

| Strong | Satisfactory | Weak |
|---|---|---|
| There is a clear, sound ABL credit culture. Board and management appetite for risk is well communicated and fully understood. | The ABL credit culture is generally sound, but the culture may not be uniform and risk appetite may not be clearly communicated throughout the bank. | The ABL credit culture is absent or materially flawed. Risk appetite may not be well understood. |
| ABL initiatives are consistent with a conservative risk appetite and promote an appropriate balance between risk taking and strategic objectives. New loan products and industries are well researched, tested, and approved before implementation. | ABL initiatives are consistent with a moderate risk appetite. Generally, there is an appropriate balance between risk taking and strategic objectives; however, anxiety for income may lead to higher-risk transactions. New products may be launched without sufficient testing, but risks are generally understood. | ABL initiatives are liberal and encourage risk taking. Anxiety for income dominates planning activities. The bank engages in new products without conducting sufficient due diligence or implementing the appropriate controls. |
| Management is effective. ABL staff possesses sufficient expertise to effectively administer the risk assumed. Responsibilities and accountability are clear. Appropriate remedial or corrective action is taken when necessary. | ABL is satisfactorily managed, but improvement may be needed in one or more areas. ABL staff generally possesses the expertise to administer assumed risks; however, additional expertise may be required in one or more areas. Responsibilities and accountability may require some clarification. In general, appropriate remedial or corrective action is taken when necessary. | ABL risk management is deficient. The ABL unit may not possess sufficient expertise or may demonstrate an indifference or unwillingness to effectively administer the risk assumed. Responsibilities and accountability may not be clear. Corrective actions are insufficient to address root causes of problems. |
| Diversification management is effective. ABL concentration limits are set at reasonable levels and risk management practices are sound, including management's efforts to reduce or mitigate exposures. Management effectively identifies and understands correlated risk exposures and their potential impact. | Diversification management is adequate, but certain aspects may need improvement. ABL concentrations are identified and reported, but limits and other action triggers may be absent or moderately high. Concentration management efforts may be focused at the individual loan level, while portfolio-level efforts may be inadequate. Correlated exposures may not be identified and their risks not fully understood. | Diversification management is passive or deficient. Management may not identify concentrations, or take little or no action to reduce, limit, or mitigate the associated risk. Limits may be present but represent a significant portion of capital. Management may not understand exposure correlations and their potential impact. Concentration limits may be exceeded or raised frequently. |
| Loan management and personnel compensation structures provide appropriate balance between loan/revenue production, loan quality, and portfolio administration, including risk identification. | Loan management and personnel compensation structures provide reasonable balance between loan/revenue production, loan quality, and portfolio administration. | Loan management and personnel compensation structures are skewed to loan/revenue production. There is little evidence of substantive incentives or accountability for loan quality and portfolio administration. |

| Strong | Satisfactory | Weak |
|---|---|---|
| ABL staffing levels and expertise are appropriate for the size and complexity of the unit. Staff turnover is low and the transfer of responsibilities is orderly. Training programs facilitate ongoing staff development. | ABL staffing levels and expertise are generally adequate for the size and complexity of the unit. Staff turnover is moderate and may result in some temporary gaps in portfolio management. Training initiatives are adequate. | ABL staffing levels and expertise are deficient. Turnover is high. Management does not provide sufficient resources for staff training. |
| ABL policies effectively establish and communicate portfolio objectives, risk limits, loan underwriting standards, and risk selection standards. | ABL policies are fundamentally adequate. Enhancement, while generally not critical, can be achieved in one or more areas. Specificity of risk limits or underwriting standards may need improvement to fully communicate policy requirements. | ABL policies are deficient in one or more ways and require significant improvements. Policies may not be clear or are too general to adequately communicate portfolio objectives, risk limits, and underwriting and risk selection standards. |
| Staff effectively identifies, approves, tracks, and reports significant policy, underwriting, and risk selection exceptions individually and in aggregate, including risk exposures associated with off-balance-sheet activities. | Staff identifies, approves, and reports significant policy, underwriting, and risk selection exceptions on a loan-by-loan basis, including risk exposures associated with off-balance-sheet activities; however, little aggregation or trend analysis is conducted to determine the effect on portfolio quality. | Staff does not identify, approve or report policy, underwriting, or risk selection exceptions or does not report them individually or in aggregate or does not analyze the exceptions' effects on portfolio quality. Risk exposures associated with off-balance-sheet activities may not be considered. |
| Credit analysis is thorough and timely both at underwriting and periodically thereafter. | Credit analysis appropriately identifies key risks and is conducted within reasonable time frames. Post-underwriting analysis may need improvement. | Credit analysis is deficient. Analysis is superficial and key risks are overlooked. Credit data are not reviewed in a timely manner. |
| Risk rating and problem loan review and identification systems are accurate and timely. Credit risk is effectively stratified for both problem and pass-rated credits. Systems serve as effective early warning tools and support risk-based pricing, the ALLL, and capital allocations. | Risk rating and problem loan review and identification systems are adequate. Problem and emerging problem credits are adequately identified, although room for improvement exists. The graduation of pass ratings may need to be expanded to facilitate early warning, risk-based pricing, or capital allocations. | Risk rating and problem loan review and identification systems are deficient. Problem credits may not be identified accurately or in a timely manner, resulting in misstated levels of portfolio risk. The graduation of pass ratings is insufficient to stratify risk for early warning or other purposes. |
| Special mention ratings do not indicate any issues regarding administration of the ABL portfolio. | Special mention ratings generally do not indicate administration issues within the ABL portfolio. | Special mention ratings indicate management is not properly administering the ABL portfolio. |
| MIS provides accurate, timely, and complete ABL portfolio information. Management and the board receive appropriate reports to analyze and understand the impact of ABL activities on the bank's credit risk profile, including off-balance-sheet activities. MIS facilitates timely exception reporting. | Management and the board generally receive appropriate reports to analyze and understand the impact of ABL activities on the bank's credit risk profile; however, modest improvement may be needed in one or more areas. Generally, MIS facilitates timely exception reporting. | The accuracy or timeliness of MIS may be materially deficient. Management and the board may not be receiving sufficient information to analyze and understand the impact of ABL activities on the credit risk profile of the bank. Exception reporting requires improvement. |

# Appendix E: Glossary

**Account payable:** A current liability representing the amount owed by an individual or a business to a creditor for merchandise or services purchased on open account or short-term credit.

**Account receivable:** A current asset representing money owed to a business for merchandise or services bought on open account. Accounts receivable arise from the business practice of providing a customer merchandise or a service with the expectation of receiving payment per specified terms.

**Advance:** A drawdown or disbursement of funds according to the terms of an existing loan agreement. Advances are common to revolving credit facilities. The term can also refer to a customer paying accounts payable before the agreed-upon date.

**Advance rate:** The maximum percentage a lender lends against a type of collateral. The advance rate varies by the type of collateral, terms, age, and sometimes the financial strength of the obligated party.

**Airball:** The portion of a loan that exceeds the amount supported by the underlying collateral and is dependent on support from the company's cash flow or enterprise value. This is also referred to as a "financing gap."

**Aging schedule:** A periodic report listing a borrower's accounts receivable or payable balances, by customer or supplier, detailing the current status or delinquency of the balances owed or owing. The report is typically used in determining the borrower's compliance with the borrowing base requirements in the loan agreement.

**Borrowing base:** A collateral base agreed to by the borrower and lender that is used to limit the amount of funds the lender advances the borrower. The borrowing base formula specifies the maximum amount that may be borrowed in terms of collateral type, eligibility, and advance rates.

**Cash burn:** The rate at which a company uses up cash. Cash burn is typically calculated as the difference between cash inflows and cash outflows for a specified period, but the calculation and adjustments may vary by borrower and bank.

**Cash dominion:** A control arrangement wherein the borrower's receivable receipts are sent by customers to a lockbox controlled by the lender. Under a full cash dominion arrangement, the bank controls the cash collections and applies the proceeds to the borrower's loan account before releasing any funds. Cash dominion relationships may also be springing. Under a springing arrangement, the cash receipts in the lockbox account are made available directly to the borrower and the bank reserves the right to control and apply the proceeds if the borrower fails to comply with the loan agreement. See **lockbox**.

**Compliance certificate:** A borrower's statement certifying adherence to the terms of the loan agreement during the stated period. The company's principal financial officer usually completes the certificate. If the borrower is in compliance with the terms of the loan agreement (i.e., no event of default has occurred), the principal financial officer attests accordingly. Supporting data is usually required to document the assertion.

**Consignment:** The physical transfer of goods from a seller or vendor to another legal entity, which acts as a selling agent for the seller. The seller, or consignor, retains title to the goods. The receiver of the goods, or consignee, acts as an agent for the consignor, sells the goods for a commission, and remits the net proceeds to the consignor. The consignor does not recognize revenue until the consignee sells the goods to a third party.

**Contra-accounts:** Situations in which an entity is both a customer and a supplier, creating accounts receivable and accounts payable that may offset each other. These accounts are usually considered ineligible collateral.

**Credit memo:** A detailed memorandum forwarded from one party or firm to another granting credit for returned merchandise, some omission, overpayment, or other cause. A credit memo may also refer to the posting medium authorizing the credit to a specific account, including details of the transaction and the signature or initials of the party authorizing the credit.

**Cross-aging:** The practice of making all of the accounts receivable from a single account party (the obligated party for an account receivable) ineligible to be included in the borrowing base if a specified proportion of the total accounts receivable from that party is delinquent. Sometimes referred to as the "10 percent rule" because 10 percent of an individual party's accounts is a common delinquency threshold.

**Cross-collateralization:** The act of securing a loan with collateral that also secures one or more additional loans. In the event of default, cross-collateralized assets are used to satisfy the collateralized debts. The terms of the agreement can also specify that only the excess collateral of one loan can be shifted to satisfy another.

**Cross-default:** The right to declare a loan in default if an event of default occurs in another loan provided to the borrower.

**Debtor-in-possession (DIP) financing:** Financing provided to a borrower after a Chapter 11 (reorganization) bankruptcy filing. A lender provides the DIP post-petition financing to support the borrower's working capital needs while the DIP attempts to rehabilitate its financial condition and emerge from bankruptcy protection. To encourage lenders to provide DIP financing, the bankruptcy code grants the DIP lender a priority claim on the DIP's assets. This provides the DIP lender protection in the event the DIP fails to emerge from Chapter 11 and liquidates. Liquidation can be accomplished by converting the case to a Chapter 7 filing.

**Dilution:** The difference between the gross amount of invoices and the cash actually collected for such invoices. Common receivable dilution factors include discounts, returns, allowances, and credit losses. The lender analyzes dilution trends as part of determining receivable advance rates.

**EBITDA:** Earnings before deduction for interest, taxes, depreciation and amortization.

**Eligible collateral:** Collateral that meets the criteria as defined term in the loan agreement for inclusion in the borrowing base.

**Excess availability:** Additional funds a borrower may draw under the terms of the credit facility. Excess availability is typically calculated as the lower of the borrowing base or loan commitment less the outstanding balance of the credit facility. Loan covenants may require a borrower to maintain a minimum amount of availability, thereby reducing the funds available. See h**ard block.**

**Field audit:** A comprehensive review of a borrower's financial reporting and operations. The scope of field audits, or exams, commonly includes reviews of the borrower's books, records, and accounting systems and inspections of collateral. Field audits are typically performed before loan origination and thereafter on a regular, often quarterly, basis as part of the ABL monitoring process.

**First-out:** a loan tranche that is pari passu with another tranche in the same facility with respect to lien rights but senior in repayment.

**Fixed charges:** Generally, the sum of capital expenditures, the current portion of long-term debt, interest, and cash taxes. Fixed charges can also include other fixed expenses and required distributions.

**Fixed charge coverage ratio:** EBITDA divided by fixed charges. This ratio measures the capacity of earnings to pay fixed charges. See **EBITDA, fixed charges**.

**Formula:** A calculation to determine the borrowing base in which a margin or advance rate is applied to each type of collateral. This may occur before or after specific reserves or blocks are considered in the borrowing base.

**Fully followed:** A term describing the process ABL lenders use to control credit availability and collateral by means of a borrowing base, control of the cash receipts, and field audits.

**Hard block:** A covenant used in an ABL revolver that establishes a minimum amount of excess availability that must be maintained at all times. The covenant can be established in a number of ways, including as a specified dollar amount or as a percentage of the borrowing base. Additional borrowing under the revolver is prohibited on violation of a hard block covenant. See **soft block.**

**Incurrence covenants:** Loan covenants that require that if a borrower takes an action (paying a dividend, making an acquisition, issuing more debt, etc.), the resulting position would need to remain in compliance with the loan agreement. For example, an issuer that has an incurrence test that limits the issuer's debt to 5x cash flow would only be able to take on more debt if, on a pro forma basis, the issuer was still within this constraint. If not, then the issuer would have breached the covenant and would be in default. If, on the other hand, an issuer found itself above this 5x threshold simply because its earnings had deteriorated, the issuer would not have violated the covenant.

**Ineligible collateral:** Pledged receivables or inventory that do not meet the criteria specified in the loan agreement. Ineligible collateral remains part of the ABL lender's collateral pool but does not qualify for inclusion in the borrowing base.

**Inventory roll-forward:** Refers to the process of using an inventory count, sales receipts, and purchases of inventory to determine the amount of inventory to roll over into the next period.

**Last-out:** a loan tranche that is equal with another tranche in the same facility with respect to lien rights but junior in repayment. The last-out tranche is typically repaid only after the first-out tranche has been fully repaid.

**Lien:** A legal right to control or to enforce a charge against another's property until some legal claim is paid or otherwise satisfied.

**Liquidation value:** The price an asset will most likely bring if the asset is sold without reasonable market exposure and when the seller is under duress. Sometimes the liquidation value is based on an orderly liquidation that allows for a brief marketing period, in contrast to a forced liquidation value that is based on an auction sale.

**Loan syndication:** The process of involving multiple lenders in providing various portions of a loan. A syndicated loan is structured, arranged, and administered by one or several commercial or investment banks known as arrangers. Syndication allows any one lender to provide a large loan while maintaining a more prudent and manageable credit exposure because the lender is not the only creditor. See **Shared National Credit Program**.

**Lockbox:** A cash management product offered by financial institutions that accelerates a client's collection of receivables. The client's customers are directed to make payments to regional post office boxes where the payments are picked up daily by the bank and processed for deposit. See **cash dominion**.

**Maintenance covenant:** Loan covenants requiring a borrower to meet certain financial tests every reporting period, usually quarterly. For example, if a borrower's loan agreement contains a maintenance covenant that limits debt to cash flow, the borrower would violate the covenant if debt increased or earnings deteriorated sufficiently to breach the specified level.

**Margin:** The difference between the market value of collateral pledged to secure a loan and the amount a bank will advance against the collateral.

**Market value:** Generally, the most likely price an asset will bring if the asset is sold in a competitive, open market, with reasonable market exposure and willing, informed buyers and sellers. Refer to the "Commercial Real Estate Lending" booklet of the *Comptroller's Handbook* for the definition of market value for loans secured by real estate.

**Net orderly liquidation value (NOLV):** The estimated value a business would receive if assets were liquidated in an orderly manner over a reasonable period, generally six to nine months. The NOLV should be established by a competent party who is independent of the credit transaction.

**Offset (set-off):** The common-law right of a lender to seize deposits owned by a debtor and deposited in the lender's institution for nonpayment of an obligation. An offset also occurs in the settlement of mutual debt between a debtor in bankruptcy and a creditor, through offsetting claims. Instead of receiving cash payment, debtors credit the amount owed against the other party's obligations to them. This allows creditors to collect more than they would under a debt repayment plan approved by a bankruptcy court.

**Operating cycle:** The period of time it takes a business to convert purchased and manufactured goods and services into sales, plus the time to collect the cash from the associated sales.

**Over-advance:** The advanced portion of a revolving credit facility that exceeds the availability calculated by the borrowing base. For example, an ABL revolver with an outstanding balance of $100 and a borrowing base of $90 is over-advanced. This term is also referred to as stretch collateral throughout ABL circles.

**Pari passu:** Credit facilities in which two or more lenders are accorded equal treatment under a loan agreement. Most frequently applied to collateral and repayment, but may also refer to loan structure, documentation, maturity, or any other substantive condition.

**Purchase money security interest (PMSI):** The interest held by sellers or third-party creditors that finance the acquisition of goods. The Uniform Commercial Code (UCC) prescribes that if a seller or creditor provides financing for a debtor to acquire specific goods, the creditor can perfect a security interest in those goods that is superior to a preexisting security interest in the same collateral. The creditor must, however, adhere to strict rules to perfect a PMSI. If the creditor violates the PMSI requirements, the creditor's lien is junior to the previously perfected financing statements.

**Receivable roll-forward:** Refers to the process for determining the volume of receivables to carry over into the next reporting period.

**Reserve:** The amount of an invoice in excess of the advance.

**Shared National Credit Program**: An interagency program to review and assess risk in the largest and most complex credits shared by multiple financial institutions. The program provides uniform treatment of and increases efficiencies in Shared National Credit risk analysis and classification. See OCC Bulletin 1998-21, "Shared National Credit Program: Description and Guidelines."

**Soft block:** An ABL revolver covenant that establishes excess availability thresholds that, when violated, permit the lender to execute springing covenants, such as minimum financial ratio standards or cash dominion. A soft block serves as a warning of potential deterioration and is always greater in amount than the hard block, should one exist. A soft block differs from a hard block in that violating the soft block does not prohibit additional borrowing under the revolver. See **hard block.**

**Uniform Commercial Code (UCC):** A model framework of laws that addresses commercial transactions. Each state may modify or exclude provisions of the model framework when adopting the UCC. While the UCC varies from state to state, the spirit of the state-adopted statutes is consistent. The UCC was established to stimulate interstate commerce by making states' commercial laws more consistent.

**Working investment:** The sum of accounts receivable and inventory, minus the sum of accounts payable and accrued expenses (excluding taxes). Working investment represents the amount of financing and trade support a company needs to fund its trading assets.

# References

## Laws

12 USC 1464(c), "Federal Savings Associations—Loans and Investments"

## Regulations

12 CFR 30 (national banks) and 12 CFR 170 (federal savings associations), appendix A, "Interagency Guidelines Establishing Standards for Safety and Soundness"
12 CFR 160, "Lending and Investment" (federal savings associations)

## Comptroller's Handbook

**Examination Process**
"Bank Supervision Process"
"Community Bank Supervision"
"Federal Branches and Agencies Supervision"
"Large Bank Supervision"
"Sampling Methodologies"

**Safety and Soundness, Asset Quality**
"Allowance for Loan and Lease Losses"
"Commercial Lending"
"Concentrations of Credit"
"Leveraged Lending"
"Loan Portfolio Management"
"Rating Credit Risk"

## OCC Issuances

Banking Circular 181 (Rev), "Purchases of Loans in Whole or in Part-Participations" (August 2, 1984)
OCC Bulletin 1998-21, "Shared National Credit Program: Description and Guidelines" (May 5, 1998)
OCC Bulletin 2007-1, "Complex Structured Finance Transactions: Notice of Final Interagency Statement" (January 5, 2007)
OCC Bulletin 2010-24, "Incentive Compensation: Interagency Guidance on Sound Incentive Compensation Policies" (June 30, 2010)
OCC Bulletin 2013-9, "Guidance on Leveraged Lending" (March 22, 2013)
OCC Bulletin 2013-29, "Third-Party Relationships: Risk Management Guidance" (October 30, 2013)

www.ingramcontent.com/pod-product-compliance
Lightning Source LLC
Chambersburg PA
CBHW052007280526
45793CB00005B/889